MacDiarmid

Open Guides to Literature

Series Editor: Graham Martin (Professor of Literature, The Open University)

Current titles

Graham Holderness: *Wuthering Heights*
P.N. Furbank: Pound
Graham Martin: *Great Expectations*
Roderick Watson: MacDiarmid

Titles in preparation include

Angus Calder: Byron
David Pirie: Shelley
Walford Davies: Dylan Thomas
Roger Day: Larkin
Jeanette King: *Jane Eyre*
Dennis Walder: Hughes
Graham Holderness: *Women in Love*

RODERICK WATSON

MacDiarmid

Open University Press
Milton Keynes · Philadelphia

Open University Press
Open University Educational Enterprises Limited
12 Cofferidge Close
Stony Stratford
Milton Keynes MK11 1BY, England

and
242 Cherry Street
Philadelphia, PA 19106, USA

First published 1985

British Library Cataloguing in Publication Data

Watson, Roderick
  MacDiarmid.—(Open guides to literature)
  1. MacDiarmid, Hugh, 1892–1978—Criticism
  and interpretation
  I. Title
  821'.912   PR6013.R735Z/

  ISBN 0–335–15090–X
  ISBN 0–335–15081–0 Pbk

Library of Congress Cataloging in Publication Data

Watson, Roderick, 1943–
  MacDiarmid.

  Bibliography: p.
  Includes index.
  1. MacDiarmid, Hugh, 1892–   —Criticism and
interpretation. I. Title.
PR6013.R735Z93   1985   821'.912   85–11539
ISBN 0–335–15090–X
ISBN 0–335–15081–0 (Pbk.)

Text design by Clarke Williams
Typeset by Cambrian Typesetters, Frimley, Surrey
Printed in Great Britain by J.W. Arrowsmith Ltd, Bristol

Dedicated to Valda and Michael Grieve
and to my good friend Norman MacCaig

Contents

Series Editor's Preface

The intention of this series is to provide short introductory books about major writers, texts, and literary concepts for students of courses in higher education that substantially or wholly involve the study of Literature.

The series adopts a pedagogic approach and style similar to that of Open University material for literature courses. *Open Guides* aim to inculcate the reading 'skills' which many introductory book in the field tend, mistakenly, to assume that the reader already possesses. They are, in this sense, 'teacherly' texts, planned and written in a manner that will develop in the reader the confidence to undertake further independent study of the topic. They are 'open' in two senses. First, they offer a three-way tutorial exchange between the writer of the *Guide*, the text or texts in question, and the reader. They invite readers to join in an exploratory discussion of texts, concentrating on their key aspects and on the main problems which readers, coming to the texts for the first time, are likely to encounter. The flow of a *Guide* 'discourse' is established by putting questions for the reader to follow up in a tentative and searching spirit, guided by the writer's comments, but not dominated by an over-arching and single-mindedly-pursued argument or evaluation, which itself requires to be 'read'.

Guides are also 'open' in a second sense. They assume that literary texts are 'plural', that there is no end to interpretation, and that it is for the reader to undertake the pleasurable task of discovering meaning and value in such texts. *Guides* seek to provide, in compact form, such relevant biographical, historical and cultural information as bears upon the reading of the text, and they point the reader to a selection of the best available critical discussions of it. They are not in themselves concerned to propose, or to counter, particular readings of the texts, but rather to put *Guide* readers in a position to do that for themselves. Experienced travellers learn to dispense with guides, and so it should be for readers of this series.

This *Open Guide* to the poetry of MacDiarmid is best used in conjunction with the two volume *Hugh MacDiarmid Complete*

Poems 1920–1972 (edited by Michael Grieve and W.R. Aitken) published by Martin Brian and O'Keeffe in 1978, and in paperback (with corrections and appendix) by Penguin in 1985. The page numbering is the same in each edition, and the *Complete Poems* page numbers are used for the poems discussed in this Guide.

Graham Martin

Acknowledgements

Grateful acknowledgement is made to the executors of the Hugh MacDiarmid estate for the use of quotations from his works. Acknowledgement is also made to Norman Allan, Edwin Smith, Charles Nicol and Duncan Glen for the photographs on pp.8, 52, 83, and 87.

My thanks go to Michael Grieve, W R Aitken, Martin Brian and O'Keeffe, and Penguin Books for *Hugh MacDiarmid Complete Poems 1920–1976*; and to the Open University for permission to develop this book from material originally contributed to their Twentieth Century Poetry course.

Finally, this book was written on a word processor, and the original OU unit was copied for me by the KDEM Optical Character Recognition machine at the Computer Service Unit of the University of Glasgow. I would like to thank this invaluable service and especially Dr Bert Welsh for his expertise. The University of Stirling Computer Unit was equally helpful, and my grateful thanks go to Angus Annan, Arlen Michaels and Rob Isbister.

Introduction: the Poetry of Hugh MacDiarmid

> I'll ha'e nae hauf-way hoose, but aye be whaur   where
> Extremes meet – it's the only way I ken   know
> To dodge the curst conceit o' bein' richt
> That damns the vast majority o' men.

These lines take us straight to the heart of MacDiarmid's life and work and to the central importance of energy and contradiction in both. MacDiarmid has always been ready to 'try his luck with the idea of chaos', and it is the variousness and vivacity of his assault on that idea that makes him unique among modern poets. At a time when so many writers and thinkers were lamenting a lack of coherence in life and art, MacDiarmid found chaos and contradiction to hold a creative promise. In this belief he took Leon Shestov, the Russian philosopher, as his 'master' and it is Shestov's conception of 'chaos' that the Scot celebrates. As early as 1922, in the first editorial of his magazine *Scottish Chapbook*, MacDiarmid deplored 'consistency' and quoted Shestov on how fear of change leads men to become 'petrified in their convictions'. Twenty years later, he reaffirmed his position with a later passage from the Russian to illustrate the essential spirit of his own work:

> The idea of chaos terrifies man, for it is assumed for some reason that in chaos, in the absence of order, he cannot live . . . In reality chaos is a lack of any order, and consequently also of that order

which excludes the possibility of life. Chaos is no limited possibility, but the direct opposite, an unlimited possibility. To grasp and admit absolute freedom is infinitely hard for us, as it is hard for a man who has always lived in darkness to look into the light.[1]

The poet rose to the existential challenge implied in Shetov's words and it is his peculiar strength and importance that he does so from within a Scottish tradition in literature and language.[2] A brief example (from *A Drunk Man Looks at the Thistle*, 1926) will suffice for the moment:

'Let there be Licht,' said God, and there was	
A little: but He lacked the poo'er	
To licht up mair than pairt o' space at aince,	once
And there is lots o' darkness that's the same	
As gin He'd never spoken	As if
– Mair darkness than there's licht,	
And dwarfin't to a candle-flame	
A spalin' candle that'll sune gang oot.	guttering
– Darkness comes closer to us than the licht	
And is oor natural element. We peer oot frae't	
Like cat's een bleezin' in a goustrous nicht	eyes; blustering
(Whaur there is nocht to find but stars	
That look like ither cats' een),	
Like cat's een, and there is nocht to find	
Savin' we turn them in upon oorsels;	
Cats canna.	

(*Complete Poems*, p.148)

This passage can be paraphrased as follows: in the face of immensity even God's light seems to be a guttering candle. Little wonder, then, that man peers into the darkness of the universe and sees only reflections of himself, and that, like a cat on a wild night, he prefers to keep under cover. But this account misses the most important element in the poem, namely the concrete comic image and the good humour conveyed by the Scots colloquial tongue. If MacDiarmid faces 'dread' at all, he does so with an affectionate irony.

The creative – Shestovian – antitheses in MacDiarmid's life are manifold. Christopher Murray Grieve was a courteous and gentle man to his many friends and yet he was also 'Hugh MacDiarmid', iconoclastic scourge of his fellow Scots and equally outspoken enemy of what he saw as the pernicious influence of English values on Scottish culture. In the late twenties he delighted in damning and disrupting bourgeois society and the literary establishment, and yet he was also serving as Town and Parish Councillor for Montrose

and as a Justice of the Peace. In those years he earned his living on
the treadmill of local journalism and still found time to write poems
of lyrical beauty. He was a life-long and politically active Socialist;
as a young reporter in 1911 he cared passionately for the struggle
of the miners in South Wales, yet at the same time he was following
an interest in astrology and theology. In 1930 he wrote:

> Better a'e gowden lyric   one golden
> Than a social problem solved
> Tho' maist folk never see
> The beauty that's evolved
> And think a million times mair
> O' their ain waugh welfare.   worthless

(From 'Better One Golden Lyric', *Complete Poems*, pp. 265–6. It is
worth noting that some editions of *A Drunk Man* and *To
Circumjack Cencrastus* give poem titles to individual sections within
the whole. These were withdrawn in later editions but remain a
useful source of reference, and may be found in the index of the
Complete Poems.)

And yet the following year he published a poem called 'First Hymn
to Lenin' which addressed the great revolutionary in these terms:

> For now in the flower and iron of the truth
> To you we turn; and turn in vain nae mair,
> Ilka fool has folly eneuch for sadness   Evèry
> But at least we are wise and wi' laughter tear
> The veil of being, and are face to face
>   Wi' the human race.

(*Complete Poems*, p.298)

Although MacDiarmid would call himself a materialist, again
and again his poetry seems to be referring to some elusive and
Platonic ideal of unity; whether it appears in the form of the vision
of a silken lady in *A Drunk Man*, or in his ideal of the 'seamless
garment' of a united and just society. Consider, for example, the
extraordinary opening to 'In the Slums of Glasgow':

> I have caught a glimpse of the seamless garment
> And am blind to all else for evermore.
> The immaculate vesture, the innermost shift,
>   Of high and low, of rich and poor,
> The glorious raiment of bridegroom and bride,
>   Whoremonger and whore,
> I have caught a glimpse of the seamless garment
> And have eyes for aught else no more.

(*Complete Poems*, p.562)

The elevated and visionary tone might belong to the Rilke of the Duino Elegies, and yet the political focus of the poem belongs very much with the writers of the mid-thirties.

MacDiarmid's poetic development is equally full of surprises. His first mature poems were brief and musical lyrics in Scots, but twenty years later he was wrestling with lengthy 'world view' poems in which a largely factual, scientific and linguistic interest expressed itself in English free verse, with long lines, an abstruse polyglot vocabulary and a distinctively didactic delivery. Yet the differences are not as fundamental as they at first appear. Let us compare, for example, a lyric published in 1926 with a few lines from a longer poem published in 1943.

Servant Girl's Bed

The tall spales	tallow gutters
And the licht loups oot,	jumps
Fegs, it's yer ain creesh	Faith; fat (flesh)
Lassie, I doot,	
And the licht that reeled	
Loose on't a wee	for a short time
Was the bonny lowe	gleam
O' Eternity.	

(*Complete Poems*, p.65)

Wherefore I seek a poetry of facts. Even as
The profound kinship of all living substance
Is made clear by the chemical route.
Without some chemistry one is bound to remain
Forever a dumbfounded savage
In the face of vital reactions.
The beautiful relations
Shown only by biochemistry
Replace a stupefied sense of wonder
With something more wonderful
Because natural and understandable.

(From 'Poetry and Science', *Complete Poems*, pp.630–1)

The lyric evokes the delicate evanescence and the beauty of flame and girl and they are both seen as brief moments of light in a prevailing darkness. (We may remember those cat's een in a goustrous nicht.) There is a medieval grimness in the suggestion that the tallow is the girl's own flesh, consumed in the very process of establishing a moment's warmth and delight for her lover. (The *memento mori* is a continuing presence in the Scottish literary tradition and, indeed, a common theme in MacDiarmid's early poems.)

In the second piece, the lyrical evocation of a perennial understanding has been replaced by a language of specific and matter-of-fact statement. These lines celebrate 'facts' and 'understanding', and they do not favour a romantic sense of 'mystery' in the individual life. Yet MacDiarmid adopts this position only to increase our sense of awe at the minute and infinite complexities of the physical world. The poem continues: 'Nature is more wonderful / When it is at least partly understood'. Thus the 'beautiful relations' are not at all out of keeping with the 'bonny lowe': whether in a scientific or a romantic mode, they both express a fundamental sense of wonder and delight.

Although the lyrical power of much of MacDiarmid's later work is diluted and perhaps even denied by its prosaic form, he remains the only modern poet of that 'first generation' who has retained a practical optimism in the attempt to encompass in its entirety what so many have taken to be a fragmented and alienating world. Eliot's 'fragments' from *The Waste Land* are not so for the later MacDiarmid, but on the contrary, each of them is a new and vitally interesting contribution to the catalogue of a believed-in wholeness (a unity devoutly pursued, even if it is ultimately unattained). The 'poetry of facts' sought by MacDiarmid was not an attempt to write poetry 'with facts in it', in the spirit of Spender's poems set in the modern industrial landscape. MacDiarmid seeks, rather, to make the reader aware of the poetry that resides *in* facts.

The multiplicity of the world and the complexity of scientific advance has never led MacDiarmid to despair, and he has never felt, as Yeats, Eliot and Auden have so often seemed to, that his is a 'shallow and blasphemous' age. In his vigorous optimism and his delight in natural detail, MacDiarmid's later work is closer in spirit to the poetry of the American Walt Whitman than it is to the work of this contemporaries. Consider, for example, these lines from Whitman:

I believe a leaf of grass is no less than the journey-work of the stars,
And the pismire is equally perfect, and a grain of sand, and the egg of
    the wren,
And the tree-toad is a chef-d'oeuvre for the highest,
And the running blackberry would adorn the parlors of heaven,
And the narrowest hinge in my hand puts to scorn all machinery,
And the cow crunching with depressed head surpasses any statue,
And a mouse is miracle enough to stagger sextillions of infidels . . .

(*Song of Myself*, 1855)

In the literature of an age characterized by a prevailing sense of dispossession and anxiety, MacDiarmid's work takes a uniquely confident and creative stance. In one sense he looks back to the Romantic individualism which assumes a privileged affinity between the poet and the mysterious face of the universe. He also believed, rather like Shelley again, that such insight was the birthright of everyone if only we could be freed from the social, political and psychological chains which bind us to a world of hypocrisy and injustice. For MacDiarmid it was Marxist Socialism that promised to liberate the masses, but he saw this as only the first step in a much greater evolutionary movement towards a 'seamless garment' woven between the spirit and the 'free impulse of life'. Thus he is a lyrical poet who came to vigorous and committed political expression: and he is a 'materialist' poet who managed to maintain a sense of awe and delight at the complexity of the physical world, and to celebrate a visionary sense of its ultimate unity.

O Ease My Spirit

O ease my spirit increasingly of the load
Of my personal limitations and the riddling differences
Between man and man with a more constant insight
Into the fundamental similarity of all activities.

And quicken me to the gloriously and terribly illumating
Integration of the physical and the spiritual till I feel how easily
I could put my hand gently on the whole round world
As on my sweetheart's head and draw it to me.

(*Complete Poems*, p.539)

MacDiarmid pursued this vision in different guises throughout an active literary career of more than thirty years. During this period it might be said that he achieved a vital new poetic 'voice' no less than three times. Thus he moved away from the undoubted success of the early Scots lyrics and *A Drunk Man* to write more poems in English with an overtly Marxist or scientific bias to them; and then, in the later thirties, he changed again, to concentrate his energies on the creation of long and abtrusely intellectual 'world language' poems such as *In Memoriam James Joyce*, which was itself only one part of a final materialist epic to be called *Mature Art*. These three periods are not absolute, of course, for the poet never entirely abandoned the publication of work in earlier modes, but they serve to identify the major movements of a long and varied creative commitment; and we will use these periods as convenient markers in our exploration of MacDiarmid's life and work.

Part One
1892–1926

Lyrics,
Metaphysics
and Polemics

He's no man ava',
And lacks a proper pride,
Gin less than a' the warld
Can ser' him for a bride! . . .

(*Complete Poems*, p.114)

While poems should speak for themselves without the intrusion of
'biographical fallacy', the broad details of a writer's life and times
do have a part to play in the story of what literature is and how it
affects us over the years. This is especially true in the case of a
writer such as Hugh MacDiarmid whose poetry and prose was
often directly addressed to the task of criticizing, redefining or
revolutionizing the cultural and political scene. Equally, the major
shifts in his creative development cannot be studied without
recognizing how they related to his own circumstances and the
years he lived through. The three 'biographical' sections spaced
throughout this book will help to provide this context to
MacDiarmid's work during his long life, for there is, after all, no
such thing as a literature or critical theory that is not itself part of
the intellectual and social world we inhabit.

"There was faur mair licht and life — o' a kind — in the hooses alang the Waterside than onywhere else in the toon." — The Esk, the "Swing bridge" and the hills above Langholm. (Photo: Norman Allan).

Readers unfamiliar with the Scots language can find some initial assistance by referring to *Appendix A*.

Early Life and the Montrose Years

Christopher Murray Grieve was born on 11 August 1892 in Langholm, a border town famous for its woollen mills. In later years he was to look back on his childhood with affection and a new understanding of 'The Muckle Toon's' influence on his imagination. Langholm sits at the confluence of three rivers – the Ewes, the Wauchope and the Esk – and 'Hugh MacDiarmid' was to write poems, essays and short stories that celebrated this landscape and the ceaseless flow of those rivers all around him:

> Sae, in the simmer time, or bricht winter days, the hooses alang the Waterside were aye fu' o' a licht and life. . . and the dunt and dirl o' the river was in them like the hert in a man, and they had shoals o' licht and the crazy castin' o' the cloods and the endless squabble o' the gulls in them faur mair even than the folk talkin' and the bairns playin'. It wasna sae much a case o' leevin' your ain life in ane o' thae hooses as bein' pairt and paircel o' the life o' the river. . . A' the ither hooses in the toon were sober and solid in comparison. And the folk that leeved in them had a guid grip o' their lives. But alang the waterside they were windy, thriftless, flee-aboot craturs. The sense was clean washed oot o' them. A' the sense – and a' the stupidity tae. It's only some kinds o' birds that ha'e een like what theirs becam' – cauld and clear and wi' nae humanity in them ava.[3]

Grieve senior was a rural postman and young Christopher grew up in the Post Office building with the Public Library and a museum on the floors upstairs. Here he formed the habits of a lifetime as a self-confessedly 'omniverous' and 'magpie' reader, and he claimed to have finished almost all the books in the place before he left home in his teens. The library was not particularly well provided with Scottish books, but bound volumes of American periodicals introduced him to the literature and history of the United States and helped him, as he put it later, 'to resist the refining influence of English education'.[4] The boy's literary bent was further encouraged by the local minister, who was a poet himself, but although his father was an elder in the United Free Church, he could not be persuaded to align himself with organized religion. Something he did share with him, however, was a taste for that 'old Radicalism. . .still strong all over the Borders'.

In 1908, at the age of sixteen, Grieve left Langholm for Edinburgh where he was to train as a schoolteacher at Broughton Higher Grade School and Junior Student Centre. Here he met

George Ogilvie, an inspired English master who was to have a considerable influence on him in later years. Ogilvie recognized his pupil's talents and, as a fellow Socialist, he introduced him to the consistent study of Scottish culture and to an eclectically intellectual London periodical, *The New Age*. Grieve blossomed in Edinburgh, where he edited the school magazine and joined the Independent Labour Party (ILP) and the University Fabian Society. After a couple of years, however, a combination of circumstances made him doubt his vocation as a teacher and prompted, too, by his father's sudden death from pneumonia at the early age of 47, the boy cut his studies short in 1911 and turned to freelance journalism. Later verses such as 'Kinsfolk', 'At My Father's Grave' and indirectly, perhaps, 'The Watergaw' were to reflect on that bereavement and on the poet's lingering sense that his father had died while the son's early promise was as yet unfulfilled.

Grieve worked as a journalist for several different papers during the next four restless years, including a spell for *The Monmouthshire Labour News* in South Wales and a term in Fife where he met Peggy Skinner, who was to become his wife. He kept a commitment to the ILP and a job in Clydebank brought him into direct contact with the socialism of men such as James Maxton and John Maclean on the home ground of what was to become known as 'Red Clydeside.' Then, in the year after war broke out, Grieve enlisted in the Royal Army Medical Corps and found himself serving as Quartermaster Sergeant in a hospital in Salonika on the 'forgotten' Eastern Front in Greece.

The young journalist kept up a correspondence with George Ogilvie and these remarkable letters testify to an extremely volatile, ambitious and doubt-ridden temperament. On fire with innumerable schemes for books, essays and sonnet sequences, Grieve was caught up by intellectual issues of every sort, passionately excited by Scottish Nationalism and, for a short while, by the Catholic faith. He also began to explore his own states of mind in a series of fictionalized 'physchological studies', begun in 1918, but not published until 1923 as *Annals of the Five Senses*. He had caught malaria shortly after arriving in Greece and it is possible that the recurring bouts of this disease may have compounded the feverish intensity of his sensibility during these early creative years. Whether this is so or not, he had to be invalided home, and during this leave in 1918 he married Peggy Skinner. Peace came while Sergeant Grieve was recuperating at a malaria centre in France and he finished his service near Marseilles at a hospital for shell-shocked Indian troops from the Western front. 'He brought back to civilization an ardour of revolt, a sharp bitterness, made up partly of hatred and partly of pity. He saw with eyes different from those of other men's – clearer or more blurred, anyhow not the same. His state of mind was grievous.' These lines from *Annals* (and the pun at the end) speak personally for the author and for so many others who survived.

Demobilized in 1919, Grieve eventually settled in Montrose as a journalist for the weekly paper and it was there that he began his literary career by editing anthologies of Scottish verse consciously modelled on Edward Marsh's earlier *Georgian Poetry* series from England. Three volumes of these *Northern Numbers* appeared between 1920 and 1922, and they included poems by John Buchan, Violet Jacob, Neil Munro and some not very good verses by the editor himself. 'Mountain Measure', for example, describing the Pyrenees in 1919, begins as follows:

> And now Aldebaran in the keen dawn dies,
> Vega and Althair from the kindly zenith pass,
> The valley mists
> Blush and dislimn
> And ancient peaks like fabulous statues stand,
> Shining like roses and athrill with song,
> Where morning burns them with apotheosis.
>
> Breastplate of Judgement, here
> The planes of man-wrought fields
> The sapphire and the agate are,
> Jasper and beryl, and their glory shines
> Like living rainbows hung about
> Th'imponderable mystery of the graven world!

(*Complete Poems*, p.1201)

The poems from this period were always in English, showing an interest in large abstractions such as Time and Death and characterized by an aureate poetic diction of clashing, jewel-hard surfaces.

Wholly committed to making his mark on literary Scotland, Grieve's next move was to found a series of periodicals, starting with a monthly *The Scottish Chapbook* (fourteen issues), which arrived in August 1922, (shortly after the publication of *Ulysses* and before the appearance of *The Waste Land*). The weekly *Scottish Nation* (thirty-four issues) began in 1923 and the following year the monthly *Northern Review* survived for only four issues. Although short-lived, these periodicals did set about the definition of a literary and political 'renaissance' in Scottish affairs. The *Chapbook* was the most influential of them all, and in October 1922 it published poems in English by its editor, C.M. Grieve, alongside some pieces in Scots by one Hugh M'Diarmid. The pen name marked his commitment to a specifically Northern culture while seeking, at the same time, 'to bring Scottish Literature into closer touch with current European tendencies in technique and ideation'. In this way Grieve was determined to break out of parochial stereotypes, and indeed, in his early years he had believed that the use of Scots for poetry was best avoided for fear of encouraging old modes or narrow antiquarianism. When his own creative experiments showed that this need not be the case, however, he became one of the language's most active propagandists. The 'Chapbook Programme' had begun, after all, with a pointed reminder from Dante that 'To make a book is less than nothing unless the book, when made, makes people anew'.

'Hugh MacDiarmid's' first collection of Scots lyrics, *Sangschaw*, appeared in 1925 and *Penny Wheep* ('small ale') was published the following year. By this time he had also completed a much larger and more ambitious work, the extended poem sequence in Scots called *A Drunk Man Looks at the Thistle*. These three volumes established him as the most exciting and innovative poet to have appeared in Scotland for over a hundred years. *Contemporary Scottish Studies* (1926), a collection of essays originally produced for *The Scottish Educational Journal*, confirmed his presence as a critic and reviewer whose journalistic expertise ensured that he could express himself forcefully, frequently and often immoderately, with an eye for the new and a fine sense of the value of controversy. At thirty-four, Hugh MacDiarmid (as we shall call him from now on), had at last achieved some of the goals he had set himself among the medical stores in Salonika, isoalted in Greece in a forgotten war ten years earlier.

Scots and the 'Scottish Renaissance'

Sergeant Grieve was one of thousands who returned to home life after the war and found it to be dull, hypocritical and sterile. Soldiers had been told that they were fighting – among other things – for the rights of Belgium and other 'small nations', and yet to many Scots it seemed as if their own small nation had become just a province of 'North Britain'. On a different front, even during the war there had been labour unrest along the Clyde because it was felt that the interests of the workers were being unduly sacrificed on behalf of a war effort controlled from London and, in 1919, a strike for a forty-hour working week raised such fears of 'Red Clydeside' that the government used troops and armoured cars to patrol the

streets of Glasgow. Scottish support for Socialism, Nationalism, or
both, was further increased when the post-war slump hit the
country's mining and ship-building industries with particular force.
The Independent Labour Party in Scotland had contained a strong
'home rule' element from the first (as had Liberal politics at the turn
of the century), and even the Communist John Maclean was
eloquent about a Scottish workers' republic which was to be free
from London and Moscow alike. Imprisoned for sedition because
of his anti-war speeches, Maclean's various trials and an early
death in 1923 made him something of a martyr and drew many
intellectuals – including MacDiarmid – to his cause.

On the cultural scene, books such as Professor Gregory Smith's
Scottish Literature: Character and Influence (1919), were to make
an equal impact on the poet, for here was a study of how a
distinctive Lowlands Scots psyche had manifested itself in the
country's literature through the centuries, from Barbour, Henryson
and Dunbar to Scott and R.L. Stevenson. By late Victorian times,
however, it seemed as if that distinguished line had degenerated to
sentimental vignettes of life in rural villages populated by pious,
crafty or droll 'Scotch worthies'. This school of writing – typified
by the 'Thrums' stories of young J.M. Barrie and the works of 'Ian
Maclaren' and S.R. Crockett – might well be condemned for its
'kailyard' (cabbage patch) parochialism, but it enjoyed a tremen-
dous vogue nevertheless, largely among urban readers, on both
sides of the Atlantic. The genre had been exploded from within in
1901 by George Douglas Brown's grimly savage novel *The House
with the Green Shutters*, but popular taste in Scotland was still tied
to a complacent vision of its own life as a matter of 'hamespun'
rustic quaintness. This was especially evident in much of the Scots
verse of the time. MacDiarmid set out to change all that.

The Scottish Chapbook sported a lion rampant on its dark red
cover, along with the slogan 'Not Traditions – Precedents!', and
although his programme supported the use of 'braid Scots', its
editor was bitterly opposed to the kailyard and all its 'pawky' and
comfortable sentiments in vernacular verse:

The Burnie

I'm but a wee bit burnie,	little stream
Ye'll agree;	
Gaun singin' on my journey,	Going
Blythe and free;	
Fu' o' fun and daffin',	frolicking
Thro' the meadows I gae lauchin',	
To the sea.	

I ca' the auld meal mill	turn (the wheel of the watermill)
Abune the toon,	Above
Then toddle doon the hill,	
An amber broon;	
Lanely on I travel	
Owre the chuckie-stanes and gravel,	
Till I reach a laigher level	lower
Far'er doon.	

MacDiarmid claimed that even the human, satirical and ribald spirit of Burns had been made 'respectable' among philistines or diluted to 'haggis and ginger beer' by a long succession of such effusions, emanating from the 'poetry corner' of innumerable local newspapers. This is the context of his rousing attack on Burns Clubs at the start of *A Drunk Man Looks at the Thistle*.

The poet grew fond of citing Hardy's definition of literature as 'the written expression of revolt against accepted things' and, in place of Burns, he made William Dunbar his champion – a sophisticated and technically dazzling court poet from the late fifteenth century – a figure far indeed from 'The Burnie' and everything it represents. At the same time, MacDiarmid declared war on Harry Lauder and all such music hall images of the 'Scotchman' as a comic and canny peasant. To complete a comprehensive brief, he opened fire as well on what he called the 'Anglo-Scottish Establishment'. These were the cultural pundits, educators, editors and reputation-makers of Scotland, whom he felt were basically hostile to their native culture, looking only to England (or, more specifically, to London) for their literary values. Thus most of the Scottish newspapers were opposed to home rule and Socialism alike, despite popular support for such movements and a national propensity for radical opinion. He pointed out that the schools and universities had skimped or neglected the teaching of Scottish literature and history for too long, while children were discouraged from using Scots in the classroom and, in the North West, even punished for speaking their native Gaelic. MacDiarmid claimed that 'English cultural imperialism' was to blame, going back to the Union of 1707, but although he listed 'Anglophobia' as his hobby in *Who's Who*, his fiercest shafts were directed against the Scots themselves, in a bid to make them culturally more self-reliant and outward-looking:

The only race in History who've

Bidden in the same category
Frae stert to present o' their story,
And deem their ignorance their glory. . .

They ca' their obstinacy 'Hame'. . .
(From '*A Drunk Man Looks at the Thistle*', *Complete Poems*, p.165)

This vigorous campaign was intended to revitalize the creative and political self-confidence of Scotland. Of course, these aims were not unique to MacDiarmid and support came from many quarters. Throughout his most hectic creative years in the 1920s, he wrote literally hundreds of articles on Scottish affairs, all designed to promote the hoped-for revival. Politics and culture became inseparable, but it is important to realize that the Scottish Renaissance was an outward-looking movement in the belief that Scotland had much to learn from and also to contribute to the wider European scene. The poet defended the cultural independence of all small nations and asserted that without such diversity there could be no true internationalism. (Contemporary concerns for minority groups, alternative technology and the belief that 'small is beautiful', have much in common with this point of view.) Other writers responded to the challenge and, by the early 1950s, several considerable poets were publishing work with a new sense of their national identity, much of it in Scots or Gaelic. MacDiarmid did not create this revival single-handedly, but he undoubtedly gave it force, direction and some of its finest poetry. It is fitting that the phrase 'Scottish Renaissance' was first coined by a French critic.

Apart from the question of nationalism, there are notable parallels between MacDiarmid's literary campaign in the Scotland of the twenties and the 'modernist' programmes in England ten years earlier. In both cases there was a reaction against a conventional poetry of rural settings (the weaker 'Georgians' and the Scottish 'kailyard') and T.E. Hulme and T.S. Eliot, like MacDiarmid, had early emphasized the importance of European influences. But if the Scottish Renaissance was to be such a *modern* revival, why did it insist on using Scots from the outset?

The Use of Scots

Early in 1923, as editor of *The Scottish Chapbook*, MacDiarmid published a three-part 'Theory of Scots Letters'. His case for Scots is complex, curious and many-sided, and he was to prosecute it for at least the next fifteen years. For present purposes it will be helpful to summarize aspects of it in a question-and-answer form, compiled from the poet's deliberations on the subject at various times. The case for Scots is a fascinating one because it makes us question the unthinking assumptions we so often make about *English*. If you come from Liverpool, central London, Bradford, Cardiff or Norwich (much less Glasgow, Aberdeen or America), you may care

to ask yourself how often the language heard in the streets corresponds to 'Standard English', or to what you read in poems.
Q To go straight to the point, Dr Grieve, is not English a better medium than Scots for a poet writing today?
A 'Any language, real or artificial, serves if a creative artist finds his medium in it. In other words, it does not depend at all upon any other consideration, but wholly upon that *rara avis*, the creative artist himself.'
Q But why use such a little known language? Doesn't it limit your audience to Scotsmen only?
A 'Some of the most powerful influences in modern European literature, Ibsen, for example, wrote in relatively little known languages, and that neither restricted their international influence nor stunted their intellectual growth.'
Q But you had a choice between English and Scots and you chose the latter. Why?
A 'To encourage the experimental exploitation of the unexplored possibilities of vernacular expression.'
Q What might these 'unexplored possibilities' be?
A 'The vernacular is a vast unutilized mass of lapsed observation made by minds whose attitudes to experience and whose speculative and imaginative tendencies were quite different from any possible to Englishmen and Anglicized Scots today.'
Q Can you say more about this, please?
A 'We have been enormously struck by the resemblance – the moral resemblance – between Jamieson's *Etymological Dictionary of the Scottish Language* and James Joyce's *Ulysses*. A *vis comica* that has not yet been liberated lies bound by desuetude and misappreciation in the recesses of the vernacular and its potential uprising would be no less prodigious, uncontrollable, and utterly at variance with conventional morality than was Joyce's tremendous outpouring.'
Q What effects, for example?
A 'A realistic practical quality – it is misleading to call it "common sense" – is the distinguished feature of the whole Scottish tradition of poetry. . . It is this which makes Professor Gregory Smith single out as one of the chief characteristics of Scottish literature that piling up of details the completed effect of which "is one of movement". . . We have gone astray if we call this art merely meticulous, a pedant's or cataloguer's vanity with words.'
Q But can creativity be found in a dictionary?
A 'There are words and phrases in the vernacular which thrill me with a sense of having been produced as a result of mental processes

entirely different from my own and much more powerful. They embody observations of a kind which the modern mind makes with increasing difficulty and weakened effect. Take the word "birth", for instance, meaning a current in the sea caused by a furious tide but taking a different course from it – a contrary motion . . . Then there are natural occurences and phenomena of all kinds . . . no words exist for them in English. For instance – "watergaw" – for an indistinct rainbow; "yow-trummle" (ewe-tremble) – meaning the cold weather in July after the sheepshearing; "cavaburd" – meaning a thick fall of snow; and "blue bore" – meaning a patch of blue in a cloudy sky. Another feature of the vernacular which I will not illustrate here is the fashion in which diverse attitudes of mind are telescoped into single words or phrases, investing the whole speech with subtle flavours of irony, commiseration, realism and humour which cannot be reproduced in English. In onomatopoetic effect, too, the vernacular has a wider range and infinitely richer resources than English. And one of the most distinctive character-istics of the vernacular, part of its very essence, is its insistent recognition of the body, the senses . . . and the reconciliation it effects between the base and the beautiful recognizing that they are complementary and indispensable to each other.'

[Look at 'The Watergaw' for two of the words mentioned above, and at 'Scunner' for something of the base. and the beautiful together. 'Gairmscoile' both discusses and demonstrates the power of those 'coarse words that shamble thro' oor minds like stots' (bullocks).]

Q   I agree that 'cavaburd' and 'blue bore' are impressive words, drawn very much, I imagine, from the countryman's eye and the physical vividness of his everyday experience. But the modern city dweller has lost much of this kind of perception and sensitivity, so what can it mean to him? And using the dictionary like this, doesn't it make your poems rather artificial?

A   Let me remind you, to come full circle, that it all depends 'upon that *rara avis*, the creative artist himself . . . Joyce has drawn upon the whole world – but what is more to the point is to note that experiments similar in kind, if not in range, to his are to be found in every literature today – more extensive foreign borrowings, syntheses from dialects, use of archaic forms . . . technical vocabu-laries, and so on.'

Q   So you believe that your use of Scots is a part of a wider modern tendency?

A   'The key to "modernist" literature lies in the recognition of. . . the extent to which modern psychological discovery has exposed the superficiality of normal usages of language and stimulated all manner of endeavours to overcome its limitations. It seems to me that Scotland can contribute notably to this. The peculiar virtues of Scots produce works which are strictly incomparable, i.e. insusceptible of comparison, with the very different products of other tongues.'

Q   So you feel that small nations have a part to play, in literature, as well as in politics?

A   Yes. But may I answer that in some lines from one of my poems? Even if it is not one in Scots.

Scotland Small?

Scotland small? Our multiform, our infinite Scotland *small*?
Only as a patch of hillside may be a cliché corner
To a fool who cries 'Nothing but heather!' where in September
        another
Sitting there and resting and gazing round
Sees not only the heather but blaeberries
With bright green leaves and leaves already turned scarlet,
Hiding ripe blue berries; and amongst the sage-green leaves
Of the bog-myrtle the golden flowers of the tormentil shining;

(*Complete Poems*, pp.1170–71)

MacDiarmid's 'answers' here are drawn from several essays, mostly from the twenties and thirties, and some of his concerns are clearly ones that were 'in the air' during the early modern period. The dialogue covers many aspects of the debate for and against the use of Scots, and this is an issue which can still rouse Scottish writers and critics to heated argument. The poet makes a notable case, however, in his insistence that language is fundamentally inseparable from psychology. That is to say, it encapsulates, or – more than that – it *is* the outlook, judgement, character and cultural history of the language user. He insists, too, that Scots can offer new things to modern literature, especially in the way in which 'diverse attitudes of mind or shades of temper are telescoped into single words or phrases, investing the whole speech with subtle flavours of irony, commiseration, realism and humour which cannot be reproduced in English'.

I have not given all the answers (nor all the questions), and you may care to debate the issue yourself, bearing in mind that the problems of vocabulary cannot be any more demanding than the problems we face without question when we read Mallarmé, or even when faced with the complexities of allusion and concept in *The Waste Land* or *Four Quartets*. (This is not to say that a good

glossary and footnotes do not help.) Of course MacDiarmid is
arguing a case for his own poetry, as well as for Scots, in the
dialogue I have constructed. Nevertheless, Scots does seem to
possess a striking colloquial vigour and image-making power. We
must move to MacDiarmid's early Scots lyrics to see how this was
borne out in practice.

The Early Lyrics

Despite the *Chapbook's* war-cry 'Not Traditions – Precedents!' the
lyrics of MacDiarmid's first two collections do have a traditional
foundation. To support this observation, one could point to the
'domestic' character of many of the poems, stemming as they do
from an unforced appreciation of the events of everyday life in a
small community. Thus 'Focherty', for example, is a poem drawn
from rural life much in keeping with the nineteenth-century 'bothy
ballads' sung and composed by farm labourers in the North East of
Scotland:

Duncan Gibb o' Focherty's	(name of his farm)
A giant to the likes o' me,	
His face is like a roarin' fire	
For love o' the barley-bree.	whisky
He gangs through this and the neebrin' shire	goes
Like a muckle rootless tree	huge

(Complete Poems, p.53)

Compare this with George Bruce Thomson's 'Macfarlan o' the
Sprotts' which is a bothy ballad bewailing the meanness and the
treacherous nature of a local farmer. Here is the chorus only:

I dinna like Macfarlan noo,I'm safe eneuch to state,	enough
His lugs wid cast a shaida ower a sax-fit gate;	ears;six-foot
He's saft as ony gorblin,bit he's sliddery as a skate	unfledged bird
Macfarlan o' the Sprotts o' Birnieboosie.	(name of farm)

This essentially good-humoured but cutting intimacy is very much a
part of the eighteenth- and nineteenth-century tradition in Scots
verse and it can be found again in such poems of MacDiarmid's as
'Crowdieknowe', 'The Last Trump', 'Bubblyjock', 'Hungry
Waters', 'In Mysie's Bed', 'Morning', 'Wild Rose', 'Parley of
Beasts', 'The Love-Sick Lass', 'Tam', 'Whip-the-World' and 'O Jesu
Parvule'.

Although many of these lyrics can be characterized as 'domestic'
in this way and most of them contain domestic elements, this is by

no means all that they have to offer. MacDiarmid's achievement was to add to this familiar background an original concern with the mysteries of life and being, and to express it through images drawn from the stars and planets. Critics have referred to this as his 'cosmic' imagery and it can be found in poems such as 'The Bonnie Broukit Bairn', 'The Eemis Stane', 'Au Clair de la Lune', 'The Innumerable Christ', 'Empty Vessel', 'Somersault', 'Reid E'en', 'The Long Black Night' and 'Krang'. 'Domestic' and 'cosmic' are the two terms most commonly used to describe the early Scots lyrics, and both qualities are frequently found in the same poem. You might like to read those poems now.

If MacDiarmid is interested in the 'mysteries of being' as I suggest, it does not mean that these poems are abstract in any way. Let us consider, for example, 'The Innumerable Christ'. Clearly this poem shows a philosophical interest, and, indeed, it owes its inspiration to a comment made by a Professor of Theology. The poem speculates on the omnipresence of the God of Love throughout the vastness of space and time. And we should note that by implication it also suggests the endless presence of human suffering and cruelty. These are large themes, to say the least, but they are made immediate, dramatic and familiar by the colloquial directness of the Scots and the simple stanza form. (For all that MacDiarmid admired Dunbar, these poems show a much clearer technical debt to the ballads, and especially to their impersonal, yet involved, narrative voice.)

The Innumerable Christ

Other stars may have their Bethlehem, and their Calvary too.
Professor J.Y.Simpson

Wha kens on whatna Bethlehems	Who knows
Earth twinkles like a star the nicht,	
An' whatna shepherds lift their heids	
In its unearthly licht?	
'Yont a' the stars oor een can see	Beyond; eyes
An' farther than their lichts can fly,	
I' mony an unco warl' the nicht	strange world
The fatefu' bairnies cry.	fateful children
I' mony an unco' warl' the nicht	
The lift gaes black as pitch at noon,	sky
An' sideways on their chests the heids	
O' endless Christs roll doon.	

An' when the earth's as cauld's the mune
And a' its folk are lang syne deid,
On coontless stars the Babe maun cry   must
   An' the Crucified maun bleed.

(*Complete Poems*, p.32)

This 'familiar' element is found in most of these poems and it does much to explain their particular and original excellence. Consider 'Somersault' for example:

Somersault

I lo'e the stishie	love; rumpus
O'Earth in space	
Breengin' by	plunging (recklessly)
At a haliket pace.	wild giddy irresponsible
A wecht o' hills	weight
Gangs wallopin' owre,	Goes; over
Syne a whummlin' sea	Then, tumbling
Wi' a gallus glower.	tough and impudent stare (or scowl)
The West whuds doon	whizzes (thuds) down
Like the pigs at Gadara,	(the Gadarene swine)
But the East's aye there	still
Like a sow at the farrow.	

(*Complete Poems*, pp.47–8)

Professor David Daiches writes of this poem that:

The similes of the last stanza startle us by their apparent incongruity, and the shock of attention that results provides that combination of cosmic geography and a sense of the earthiness of physical life – the midden heap linked to the stars, and *both equally there* – that is at the core of so much of MacDiarmid's poetry.[5]

Let us consider the terms we have dealt with so far and apply them to a specific poem as an exercise. Read 'The Eemis Stane' and try to answer the questions I raise before going any further.

The Eemis Stane

I' the how-dumb-deid o' the cauld hairst nicht	harvest
The warl' like an eemis stane	ill-poised
Wags i' the lift;	sky
An' my eerie memories fa'	
Like a yowdendrift.	ground blizzard

Like a yowendrift so's I couldna read
The words cut oot i' the stane
Had the fug o' fame   moss
An' history's hazelraw   lichen
No yirdit thaim.   buried

(*Complete Poems*, p.27)

(a)   In what way is the poem 'domestic' or 'cosmic'; 'abstract' or
      'concrete'?
(b)   What is the central image of the poem and does it develop?
(c)   What are the poet's memories? Can we infer anything about
      them or about his mood? What is the poem 'about'?

DISCUSSION

(a)   Clearly the poet's vision might be said to have a cosmic scope
when he sees the planet as though it were a tilting stone in the sky.
Yet this experience occurs on a cold harvest night, a homely enough
setting. In the same way, the abstractions of 'fame' and 'history' are
reduced to a small scale and made familiar in those striking
metaphors of moss and lichen.

(b)   The central image of the poem – the eemis stone – develops in
the second stanza into an inscribed stone, covered with moss. To
me, this strongly suggests a grave-stone. This rather sombre
association can be supported by the poem's prevailing mood. It is
set in the depths of a cold night and the Scots idiom 'how-dumb-
deid' brings death and silence to our minds in the very first line. The
poet's memories are not specified, but they, too, are appropriately
'eerie'. In the same vein, the harvest is a fruitful image, but moss
and lichen thriving slowly on stone provide a more disturbing
image of growth and age.

(c)   Thus, even although we cannot specify the poet's memories,
their grim mood is becoming clearer. They swirl like a blizzard
(another image of coldness) and they obscure whatever message the
world might have had for him, even supposing that the accretions
of history and time had not already buried it beyond sight. It may
be that it would have been an epitaph, were it deciphered. For the
rest, the night is cold, dead and without speech. At a time of harvest
the world seems insecure. All man's fame and achievements are no
more than moss on a rock.

The poem creates a most powerful mood, and although its
images are concrete enough, in the end they suggest only a larger
and unfathomable mystery. Yet the verse is simple, musical and
direct in its execution. Kenneth Buthlay admires the image-making
power of these lyrics, and as an example he mentions the poem
'Morning' in which MacDiarmid sees the sun as being popped into

the sky by a housewifely 'Day', as though she were dropping a frog into a cream jug.

Morning

The Day loups up (for she kens richt weel	jumps; knows very well
Owre lang wi' the Nicht she mauna lig)	Too long, must not lie
And plunks the sun i' the lift aince mair	in the sky
Like a paddle-doo i' the raim-pig.	frog; cream jug

(*Complete Poems*, p.58)

Buthlay notes in passing that this effect is similar to that sought by T.E. Hulme and the Imagists and as this is an illumating observation I would like to develop it further.[6]

Most of MacDiarmid's lyrics retain a ballad-like form, quite unlike the Imagist *vers libre* experiments of ten years earlier; nevertheless, many of them do meet the various Imagist 'rules' with considerable success. For example, they are succinct, they do give, as Ezra Pound sought, a 'direct treatment of the "thing" whether subjective or objective'; they are very concentrated and they 'produce poetry that is hard and clear, never blurred nor indefinite'. Finally, at least to someone familiar with the Scottish tradition in literature, they 'use the language of common speech', employing 'always the exact word, not the nearly-exact, nor the merely decorative word'. It should be realized in this context that although some of MacDiarmid's words might puzzle native Scots speakers, the bias of the language is still unmistakeably popular. More than this, however, MacDiarmid was using 'image-making' qualities native to the language and already present in its vocabulary. Let us consider 'Morning' more closely for example.

Surely that 'paddle-doo' in the cream jug is a most incongruous combination, a striking, even a disturbing image in the manner of the first line of Pound's poem 'L'Art, 1910'? ('Green arsenic smeared on an egg-white cloth'.) Yet the *Scottish National Dictionary* tells us that in the past some country folk (apparently) kept a live frog in the cream jar so that its movements could help make butter. And because it gets white with the milk it might be referred to as a pigeon, or indeed, a 'paddle-dove'. So what at first acquaintance may seem like a deliberately grotesque image, turns out to be a part of traditional folk practice, or at least of folk lore. This is exactly what MacDiarmid meant when he claimed that the Scots language contained an 'unutilized mass of lapsed observation' and, indeed, a '*vis comica* that has not yet been liberated'.

We might class 'Morning' as a 'domestic' poem, except that the

goodwife in it is a personification of Day and that the frog in the jug
is no less than the sun itself – a far cry from Phoebus Apollo and his
chariot! Consider the poem again in the light of this precept from
the Preface to the 1915 edition of *Some Imagist Poets*:

> To present an image. . . We are not a school of painters, but we
> believe that poetry should render particulars exactly and not deal in
> vague generalities, however magnificent and sonorous. It is for this
> reason that we oppose the cosmic poet, who seems to us to shirk the
> real difficulties of his art.

The uniqueness of MacDiarmid's achievement is to have rendered
even the cosmic in a 'particular', 'exact' and earthily familiar way,
and the Scots language and its embedded world-view has made a
most vital contribution. One more example will make this clear.

Let us compare T.E. Hulme's poem 'Autumn' with MacDiarmid's
'Moonstruck'. Make this an exercise for yourself in the light of
what has been said so far, before moving on to the discussion
below. What points of similarity do you notice?

Autumn

A touch of cold in the Autumn night –
I walked abroad,
And saw the ruddy moon lean over a hedge
Like a red-faced farmer.
I did not stop to speak, but nodded;
And round about were the wistful stars
With white faces like town children.

Moonstruck

When the warl's couped soon' as a peerie   smooth as a spinning top
That licht-lookin' craw o' a body, the moon,
Sits on the fower cross-win's   crosswinds
Peerin' a' roon'.   all round

She's seen me – she's seen me – an' straucht   straightaway
Loupit clean on the quick o' my hert.   jumped
The quhither o' cauld gowd's fairly   beam; cold gold
Gi'en me a stert.

An' the roarin' o' oceans noo'
Is peerieweerie to me;   very small sound
Thunner's a tinklin' bell: an Time
Whuds like a flee.   drones by

(*Complete Poems*, p.24)

DISCUSSION

The strength of 'Autumn' lies in its directness. Each of the two central images has a sentence to itself and these sentences make up the whole poem. The similes have to do with the look of the moon and stars (ruddy and white 'faces') but looked at more closely, they convey more about the quality of the experience than about appearances. Thus the moon is bucolic, at ease and, contrary to its traditional aspect, it is masculine. The poet gives it a nod, acknowledging and respecting its presence (and its curiosity, perhaps) but he does not seek further contact. The stars, on the other hand, seem to plead for more attention. They are 'wistful', out of place among the hedgerows, and, unlike the ripe autumn moon, they seem thinner, smaller and paler, bringing a hint of winter to come.

The poet's plain statements – 'a touch of cold' and 'I did not stop to speak' – contract effectively with the unexpected last two lines. These do not follow logically from his encounter with the moon even although they are introduced by 'and'. In this way the poem leaves us with an impression rather than a conclusion. In effect, the second image opens the poem up again when the first simile seemed to have concluded it. The 'quality' of the experience might be summed up as follows. We feel the fullness of the autumn night and yet there is a sense of longing there; we feel the poet's reserve, a hint of harder times and the sense that somehow he is being observed and that something more is being asked of him – 'a touch of cold', indeed. You will also notice that the poem moves much faster and more neatly than my description of it: the 'image', in Pound's words, 'presents an intellectual and emotional complex in an instant of time'.

Like Hulme, MacDiarmid personifies the moon in his poem, but he animates it even more vividly by a striking piece of wit. The phrase 'licht-lookin' craw o' a body' links familiarity with disdain exactly as one of the gossips in 'The Bonnie Broukit Bairn' might talk and this is because 'licht-lookin' implies a person of little weight or importance, as well as referring to the moon's reflected light. A 'craw o' a body' is similarly jocular and derisive, until we notice that the silver moon (traditionally romantic and feminine), is being compared to a crow. No sooner do we recognize the witty reversal in this metaphor than MacDiarmid reverses it again and re-establishes the moon's glamour in the second stanza; and then in the third he moves on to his own response. Thus the poem moves swiftly and disconcertingly from image to image, from crow to beam of gold to tinkling bell, and especially to that last and most striking combination of the abstract and the concrete with onomatopoeic effect: 'Time whuds like a flee'. Images are used more swiftly and much more intensively in 'Moonstruck' than in 'Autumn', and in this respect, MacDiarmid is more prodigal than any of the Imagist poets I know. (The opening line alone might make the conclusion to an acceptable poem!)

This vigorous pace is typical of MacDiarmid's work in Scots, largely created by the combination, as well as the contradiction, of his images, many of which derive from the colloquial character of the language itself. Thus, for example, in using the *Scottish National Dictionary* to verify 'craw o' a body' as a term of contempt, I came across this expression. 'Is there no enough sense amang ye to licht the lamp? Sittin' there like craws i' the mist'. Surely this is a picture that any Imagist would have been delighted to create? Of course, the Imagist aims and experiences were different, but it is still instructive to note that they did not turn to popular speech in the way that MacDiarmid did, despite the value they placed on colloquial ease and authenticity of expression. This Elizabethan vigour of expression is at the heart of what MacDiarmid felt that Scots could contribute to the 'modernist' experiments in literature. (Look again at his remarks on this in the 'interview' above.) Joyce had the richnesses of Dublin speech; but Yeats' colloquialisms are a mannered affair, and Eliot had nothing equivalent to the vernacular resources of Scots to draw on.

The matter goes deeper, for Scots also contributed a certain 'estrangement' to these poems, and this effect can be felt even by native speakers. That is to say, our habitual linguistic responses and expectations are 'defamiliarized' and we are made freshly sensitive to the oddness of words and their world. This is the main subject of poems such as 'Tarras' (p.337) and 'Gairmscoile' (p.72: it means 'language-school' in Gaelic) in which the guttural and 'rumgunshoch' (rough) words take over the poems and dominate them with their speech-noises. 'Tarras', for example, celebrates a 'Bolshevik bog', the unglamorous broken ground in so many of Scotland's wilder parts, which the poet woos as if it were some monstrous female lover – the doup [arse] of the world is under you here'. While still in the line of Romantic landscape description, the aggressively odd words make those conventions strange and ugly and newly bright again – a reconciliation of 'the base and the beautiful', indeed:

The fog-wa' splits and a gair is set	fog-wall;patch of green hillside
O' corbie oats and corcolet	black oats and lichen
And drulie water like sheepeik seeps	muddy; sheep-grease

Through the duffie peats, and cranglin' creeps,	spongy; winding
Crowdles like a crab, syne cowds awa'. . .	crawls; floats slowly

(*Complete Poems*, p.338)

Such linguistic 'estrangement' shakes our complacency about how we understand words.

In this fashion 'Tarras' and 'Water Music' (p.333) made positive use of vernacular resources to match Joyce's *avant-gardeism* and Pound's demand to 'make it new'. However, MacDiarmid's concern with such effects is more than linguistic. He was regularly drawn to explore the nature of those disconcerting moments of mystery and terror when something unknowable passes between the individual and the world at large. (Remember 'Moonstruck', for example). Such feelings are inherent in his 'cosmic' view (as in 'The Eemis Stane'), but MacDiarmid also finds them in the loving relationships between people. The latter mood can be found in a poem already mentioned, 'Servant Girl's Bed'; in 'The Watergaw' (p.17), which deals with a loved-one's death, and it is seen superbly in 'Empty Vessel', where a mother's love for her lost child becomes at one with the light that curves through space, and surpasses even that all-embracing illumination. (In his essay 'Between Any Life and the Sun', George Bruce notes that MacDiarmid borrowed the situation and the first line of this poem from a traditional song in an eighteenth-century collection, and then he goes on to point out that 'the licht that bends owre a' thing' is quite in keeping with the abstruse concepts of Einsteinian physics.)[8] Other poems of this sort include 'In the Hedge-Back', 'Reid E'en', 'The Widower' and especially 'The Quest' and 'Scunner'. 'The Quest' and 'In the Hedge-Back' hint at the sense of strangeness, immensity and timelessness to be found in a lover's arms. 'Scunner' makes this theme explicit, and yet recognizes at the same time our physical frailties and limitations, and the appetites that make for disgust as well as beauty, as a part of love. As an example of this compare 'Scunner' and 'Empty Vessel' (pp.64, 66).

We have looked at MacDiarmid's Scots lyrics and discovered in them elements of the 'domestic', the 'cosmic' and the 'mysterious'. There now remains one other equally striking quality which is present in all these terms and which makes, at the same time, a category in itself. I will call this last aspect 'energy', and it should be already familiar from poems such as 'Moonstruck', 'Morning' and 'Somersault' with their vigorous juxtapositions of unusual images. It is through such juxtapositions that MacDiarmid animates the landscapes of his lyrics again and again with an almost hallucinatory, or even expressionist intensity. This can be found in such poems as 'Overinzievar', 'Ex Vermibus', 'Wheelrig', 'Country Life', 'Cloudburst and Soaring Moon', 'Somersault', 'The Fairmer's Lass', 'Sunny Gale', and 'Krang'. Let us look at two poems as examples of what I mean. First, 'On an Ill-Faur'd Star', published in 1923, but only recently collected; and next 'Farmer's Death'.

On an Ill-Faur'd Star   ugly, ill-favoured

Far aff the bawsunt mountins jirk	white streak (on cow or horse's face)
Their kaims o' ribie trees.	hillcrest or cockscomb;tall,scrawny
Like howlets roostin' roon' aboot	owls; crying roughly
Are a' the seas.	
Ae rimpin' i' the riach lan'	One lean cow; dun-coloured
Glowers at the lift revure:	sky; scornful, gloomy
An' yont its muckle ringle-een	beyond; great wall eyes
Time scuds like stour.	lashes past (as in rain in wind); dust (or water in wind)

(*Complete Poems*, p.1233)

The landscape of this poem is portentously, even violently, animated and the rough, alliterative Scots gives it an added harshness. The mountains are streaked with white (snow), like the white on the face of animals and they 'jerk' the trees on them like a cock shaking its wattles. The seas screech all around like owls. The only truly living thing here is a starved and wall-eyed cow which glares at the sky while Time lashes past like dust in a storm. The animate and inanimate interpenetrate to such an extent in this poem that the cow and the mountains seem equally active components of a tormented and Gothic world. In fact, every aspect of this 'ill-faur'd' place has been steeped in the poet's own sense of dread and unfocused intensity. This is why I suggested that some of the lyrics have Expressionist force.

'Expressionism' is an approach to art that dislocates and distorts the 'everyday' aspect of the world, and by its concentration on unusual and even abnormal states it attempts to convey something of the artist's inner experience and his relationship with the world. Strictly speaking, 'Expressionism' as a 'movement' originated among the arts in Germany in the years directly before and after the First World War. Eliot's *The Waste Land* is the most striking example of this mode in English along with parts of Joyce's *Ulysses*. Or consider, for example, these lines from Eliot's 'Rhapsody on a Windy Night':

Half-past three,
The lamp sputtered,
The lamp muttered in the dark.
The lamp hummed:
'Regard the moon,
La lune ne garde aucune rancune, (the moon bears no grudge)
She winks a feeble eye,
She smiles into corners.
She smooths the hair of the grass.
The moon has lost her memory.
A washed-out smallpox cracks her face,
Her hand twists a paper rose,
That smells of dust and eau de Cologne,
She is alone
With all the old nocturnal smells
That cross and cross across her brain.'[9]

Both Eliot's and MacDiarmid's poems convey highly coloured and apocalyptic moods and they both use vividly concrete and grim images in unusual combinations – 'Like howlets . . . are a' the seas' and 'She smooths the hair of the grass'. In the light of this comparison, several of MacDiarmid's lyrics might be said to be Expressionist, and, indeed, he once expressed an admiration for the 'grotesquerie' he had found in the work of several of the Expressionists in Germany.

As an exercise, consider this next poem, 'Farmer's Death', as an Expressionist piece.

Farmer's Death

Ke-uk, ke-uk, ke-uk, ki-kwaik,	
The broon hens keckle and bouk	brown,cackle;swell (their feathers)
And syne wi' their yalla beaks	then
For the reid worms houk.	dig, burrow
The muckle white pig at the tail	end
O' the midden slotters and slorps,	dunghill/refuse heap;gobbles
But the auld ferm hoose is lown	farmhouse; hushed, undisturbed
And wae as a corpse.	woeful
The hen's een glitter like gless	eyes; glass
As the worms gang twirlin' in,	go
But there's never a move in by	within
And the windas are blin'.	
Feathers turn fire i' the licht,	
The pig's doup skinkles like siller,	buttocks; silver
But the auld ferm hoose is waugh	bad, digusting to smell
Wi' the daith intill her.	inside it

> Hen's cries are a panash in Heaven,   hat plume (Fr. *panache*)
> And a pig has the warld at its feet;
> But wae for the hoose whaur a buirdly man woe; well-built, stalwart
> Crines in a windin' sheet.   Shrivels

(*Complete Poems*, p.34)

Here are some points to mull over before proceeding further.

(a)   The animals are more than just 'alive' while their master is dead, aren't they? How does MacDiarmid convey this?

(b)   How is the vitality of the poem expressed, to what activity does it apply?

(c)   What contrasts do you find in the poem's structure and in the images it uses. (Look at the way each stanza is put together.)

DISCUSSION

(a)   Notice the poet's use of colour in the farmyard – brown, yellow, red, white, fire, silver; and notice, too, the intense activity of the animals. The hens cackle and scrape, the pig gobbles greedily and it seems that they own the whole world, and flaunt themselves at heaven too, because their master is dead. All this creates a special vitality in the scene.

(b)   And this vitality is expressed in the act of eating, as the animals feed with the single-minded drive of that hen whose eyes are hard, bright and unfeeling as glass. Do the worms go twirling into the ground, thus sharing the energy of the scene? Or are they twirling down the hen's throat in an orgy of consumption? Either reading is acceptable, I think. Notice how the pig, too, 'slotters and slorps' with a magnificently onomatopoeic appetite.

(c)   Finally, the intensity of the poem is still further heightened by the striking juxtaposition of the images – feathers turning to fire in the glare of the day, the pig's backside shining like silver. And against the brightness and noise of the farmyard, the poet sets the stillness and the darkness of the house to make a vivid contrast in the second half of every stanza after the opening one.

Hugh MacDiarmid's first two collections established his reputation as a poet of considerable achievement. His early lyrics are regarded as his best work by several critics, among them two very fine contemporary poets, Sorley Maclean, and Iain Crichton Smith, who write both in Gaelic and English. Other readers would rate the later poetry more highly,[10] but this is what Crichton Smith has to say about the Scots poems in his essay 'The Golden Lyric'.

> Poets of course will always undervalue poems like these because they
> are so small but they are making a great mistake. The only authority

poetry ultimately has is the imagination. If we cannot claim this power and see it now and again in action how can we defend ourselves against science? When the ideas in the poem are detachable they can be contradicted and often are. MacDiarmid can be contradicted when one discusses his *In Memoriam James Joyce* (1955). He cannot be attacked at all on the level of these lyrics. They are the real proof of his genius. Their loss would be irreparable. The loss of much else of his work would not be.

The lyrics cannot be duplicated anywhere else in literature. In no other lyrics do I find their special combination of imaginative power, tenderness, wit, intelligence (but an intelligence which has not been divorced from the feelings). Clearly it would be difficult to sustain this achievement. However, though it is clear that it was necessary for MacDiarmid to move on, this does not prevent us saying that his lyrics are his greatest achievement. I can imagine most of his other work as being in a certain sense, unnecessary, that is poetically unnecessary. The lyrics made themselves necessary. They appeared through him.[11]

For myself, when trying to think of poems that move me as these lyrics do, I recall some of Hardy's poems and (the comparison may surprise), Wordsworth's 'Lucy' poems. Look again at 'Empty Vessel', 'The Eemis Stane' and 'The Watergaw' and then read Hardy's 'The Voice' and 'The Self-Unseeing' and Wordsworth's 'She dwelt among the untrodden ways' and 'A slumber did my spirit seal'. No doubt Professor Frank Kermode was prompted by a similar insight when he noted that 'MacDiarmid's early poems hid a lot of Hardy in their heather and thistle garments'.[12] But this is not the whole story either, and I think that Kermode's comment does less than justice to MacDiarmid, and least of all to the powerful expressionist fluidity in some of his lyrics. More than this, it seems to assume that the independent and active part which any language plays in creative expression were no more than a matter of donning the superficial trappings of nationalism. But what Mac-Diarmid discovered in the vernacular was the linguistic estrangement that we have been discussing, and a voice that could telescope 'diverse attitudes of mind or shades of temper. . . into single words or phrases'. All at once, this gave him access to an extraordinary creative and philosophical confidence, and its success can best be judged by comparing for yourselves the brittle and abstracted diction of that early poem 'Mountain Measure' (see p.11 above), with, say, 'The Eemis Stane'. Both poems deal with 'Th'imponderable mystery of the graven world', but the later one has gained an expressive and conceptual force that has nothing to do with 'heather' or 'thistles'. On the other hand, in his next and for some his greatest book, MacDiarmid brought the mobility of his muse into direct contact with that thistle, and the thorny questions of national stereotype and national identity.

'A Drunk Man Looks at the Thistle'

I began this study by suggesting that MacDiarmid's optimism and vigour make him unique among his contemporaries. It is, above all, in the poem *A Drunk Man Looks at the Thistle* that these qualities stand out. David Daiches has suggested that it has more in common with Chaucer, Dunbar and Villon than with Eliot, Yeats or Auden, and, indeed, many of its passages are reminiscent of the Goliardic tradition:

> Ilka pleesure I can ha'e
> Ends like a dram ta'en yesterday,
>
> And tho' to ha'e it I am lorn   longing
> – What better 'ud I be the morn?. . .

(*Complete Poems*, p.110)

'Modern' or 'Medieval', the fact is that *A Drunk Man* is an extraordinarily original and various poem. It has all the contradictions, repetitions and surprises that we associate with the modernist technique of 'stream of consciousness', and yet it is held together by essentially simple rhyme schemes and bold metres. It wrestles with philosophical abstractions, and yet it expresses them with the direct colloquial familiarity of Scots:

> For nocht but a chowed core's left whaur Jerusalem lay
> Like aipples in a heap!. . .

(p.112)

> By whatna cry o' mine oot-topped
> Sall be a' men ha'e sung and hoped
> When to a'e note they're telescoped?
>
> And Jesus and a nameless ape
> Collide and share the selfsame shape
> That nocht terrestrial can escape?

(p.160)

A Drunk Man is too substantial for any brief account and it is bound to be confusing for new readers, especially if Scots is unfamiliar to you. What follows will give some idea of its character, and you should try to read the whole poem at least once before going any further. Read it swiftly without worrying if you cannot understand some passages. At this stage it is more important to gain an overall impression. These notes will trace some of the poem's most important elements and you should take a second look at the passages referred to before turning to the discussion of them that follows.[13]

The poem's setting is simple enough. The hero is on his way home to his wife Jean, after a night out with his cronies Cruivie and Gilsanquhar. Drunk, tired and overstimulated, he falls to rest on a hillside beneath a large many-headed thistle. Under the deceptive moonlight and his intoxicated gaze, the thistle seems to change shape constantly, and as he muses on its presence it comes to stand for himself, his country, and the plight of all humankind – comic, profound, or menacing by turns. Afloat on the stream of his own consciousness, the drunk man gives himself up to these various insights, yet they are all linked by the leitmotifs of his own beliefs and preoccupations. Thus the images of thistle, rose, sea serpent, woman, whisky and moonlight take up symbolic roles and provide a thematic coherence to the poem as it follows the ebb and flow of its protagonist's rambling thoughts. Our shared introspective journey is complex, many-sided and full of contradictions, for as the voyager himself insists – 'I've nae faith in ocht I can explain'. Here again the poet's admiration for Shestov provides us with a useful starting point, for he quoted the following passage in the very first editorial of *The Scottish Chapbook*:

> Men are terrified even to appear inconstant in their own eyes. They are petrified in their convictions and no greater shame can happen to them than that they should be forced to admit that they have altered in their conviction. . . .One need neither see nor hear nor understand what is taking place around one: once your mind is made up, you have lost your right to grow; you must remain a stock, a statue, the qualities and defects of which are known to everybody.[14]

The 'right to grow' through inconsistency and to accept the 'idea of chaos' as a creative challenge – these are the ideals that MacDiarmid and his protagonist set against the cliché of the 'canny Scot', and all the bourgeois virtues of an age increasingly circumscribed by post-war depression and dour materialism. It is the freedom to 'be yourself' in Shestov's terms that the drunk man proclaims –

> To be yersel's – and to mak' that worth bein',
> Nae harder job to mortals has been gi'en.

(p.107)

Water is a recurring symbol for this theme of freedom. Early in *A Drunk Man* , he makes the following prayer:

> Like staundin' water in a pocket o'
> Impervious clay I pray I'll never be,
> Cut aff and self-sufficient, but let reenge
> Heichts o' the lift and benmaist deeps o' sea.   sky; inmost

(p.88)

From these heights he pours scorn on the 'self-sufficiency' and the 'complacency' of his fellow Scots whose failings seem to be personified by the 'Burns cult'.

> I widna gi'e five meenits wi' Dunbar
> For a' the millions o' ye as ye are.

(p.107)

For an idea of the poem's characteristic movement, you should re-read its opening sequence, from 'I amna' fou'. . .' (p.83) to '. . .A Phoenix in Paradise!' (p.99). Here are some questions for consideration.

(a)   How would you describe this kind of poetry?
(b)   Is it important that the protagonist is drunk? And if so, why?
(c)   What does his drunkenness do for the poem and do we expect to find sense in it?

DISCUSSION

(a)   The broad satirical address of the opening passage suggests that the poem is an extended dramatic monologue. Since the speaker is 'drunk', this would explain why he wanders from subject to subject, ringing the changes from music hall comedy to lyrical intensity and back to hiccups. In fact, the personality (and the condition) of MacDiarmid's drunk dominates the poem. Does this mean, then, that what he has to say must be limited and garbled?
(b)   I would suggest that it doesn't, because the drunk man's sensations go beyond those of a single individual and he is only 'poetically' drunk, after all. Thus he finds within himself a universe of human experience, and becomes, indeed, a microcosm of the universe on his own:

> Lay haud o' my hert and feel
> Fountains ootloupin' the starns   stars
> Or see the Universe reel

Set gaen' by my eident harns,   continually busy brains
Or test the strength o' my spauld   shoulder
The wecht o' a' thing to hauld!   weight of everything

(p.99)

Or again, later, he announces that:

Man's mind is in God's image made,
And in its wildest dreams arrayed
In pairt o' Truth is still displayed.

(p.158)

(c)   The whole poem proceeds from this unmistakeably Romantic
premise, as if the hero were sharing something of Walt Whitman's
confidence when he embraced all America and all humanity in
'Song of Myself'. In this context the protagonist's drunkenness has
undoubtedly released his inhibitions, but, more importantly, the
whisky in his blood has served to release his imagination too. If he
has wild hallucinations, like Tam o' Shanter, as he lies on the
hillside, he also has visions of beauty and power, like Thomas the
Rhymer on Huntley bank. In fact his drunkenness is no less than a
Dionysian intoxication, and as such it is the fount of dream,
nightmare, fantasy, obscenity, heightened awareness, free associ-
ation and all the violent and abrupt changes of mood and style
which so characterize the poem. Neither Coleridge, De Quincey nor
Rimbaud could have hoped for more from their various stimulants:

Yet but fer drink and drink's effects,
The yeast o' God that barms in us,   ferments
We micht as weel no' be alive.
It maitters not what drink is ta'en,
The barley bree, ambition, love,   whisky
Or Guid or Evil workin' in's
Sae lang's we feel like souls set free
Frae mortal coils and speak in tongues
We dinna ken and never wull   do not know
And find a merit in oorsels

(p.127)

Modern whisky may not be up to this, the original *spiritus*:

The sun's sel' aince, as sune as ye began it,
Riz in your vera saul. . .

(p.83)

It is appropriate that the drunk man should take his place in the company of Burns' Tam o' Shanter and True Thomas of the ballad, because his specific Scottishness was very important to his creator, and indeed the redefinition of national identity in a 'Theory of Scots Letters' had been one of his *Chapbook*'s main aims. A digression is in order here.

It has been suggested that Scottish literature through the ages is characterized by two contradictory moods. These were, on the one hand, a delight in down-to-earth 'matter of factness' and the accumulation of prosaic and realistic detail; and, on the other hand, a recurring appreciation of the wildest of fantasy, exaggeration and grotesquerie of all kinds. It was Professor Gregory Smith[15] who had first suggested in a light-hearted way that this *combination of opposites* might be called 'the Caledonian antisyzygy'. MacDiarmid seized upon this ironically pedantic phrase because it agreed so closely with his understanding of Scottish psychology, and without doubt his own mental processes, too. He became fond of quoting from Whitman's 'Song of Myself' – 'Do I contradict myself? / Very well then, I contradict myself, / (I am large, I contain multitudes)'; and in the 'Theory of Scots Letters' he used 'antisyzygy' to define the difference between the 'True Scot' and the 'False Scot'. The latter was everything canny and dour in the music hall stereotype, but the 'True Scot' is a Dionysian creature who has more in common with Dostoyevsky's romantically torn and divided characters than with the homespun creations of Harry Lauder or Will Fyfe. According to this theory the 'True Scot' is '. . .dominated by the conception of infinity, of the unattainable, and hence. . . ever questioning, never satisfied, rationalistic in religion and politics, romantic in art and literature (*The Scottish Chapbook*, I, 8, March 1923, p.214) MacDiarmid's theory may be debatable, but there is little doubt that his conception comes best alive in the personality of a drunk man who would 'ha'e nae hauf-way hoose, but aye be whaur / Extremes meet'.

It may be that a combination of opposites cannot be sanely sustained for long, and that because of this method, *A Drunk Man* comes to seem merely confusing and repetitious. You may already have felt this to be the case. Familiarity will make it easier, of course, but if I had to defend the poem's sometimes wayward progress, I would point to the many moments when unlikely combinations of styles and images *do* produce a vivid synthesis of poetic insight. Consider the following lines where vulgarity and spiritual longing come together, and be on the look-out for other examples of this effect in the poem:

I tae ha'e heard Eternity drip water   too
(Aye water, water!), drap by drap
On the a'e nerve, like lichtnin', I've become   one nerve
And heard God passin' wi' a bobby's feet   policeman's
Ootby in the lang coffin o' the street
– Seen stang by chitterin' knottit stang
      loup oot   paroxysm; shivering
Uncrushed by th' echoes o' the thunderin' boot,
Till a' the dizzy lint-white lines o' torture made   flax-white
A monstrous thistle in the space aboot me,
A symbol o' the puzzle o' man's soul

   (p.147)

Few modern poems work in quite this way, where spiritual anguish
is expressed with colloquial humour, and satire and religious
intensity come together in that extraordinary image of the
thundering boot of a Calvinist policeman God. Again, MacDiarmid
uses racy and straightforward rhyme schemes, and yet, at the same
time, his verses can be sensitive and moving. A Caledonian
antisyzygy, indeed: and the final irony may be that it owes not a
little of its force to a Scottish penchant for the vivid sermon! But let
us return to the poem.

   Look again at the lyrical passage in italics that begins '*At
darknin' hings abune the howff*' (pp.88–89). And look, too, at the
shorter passages in similar vein that begin '*I hae forekent ye.!*'
(p.90) and '*The Mune sits on my bed the nicht unsocht*', (pp.95–6).
(a)   What do you make of these moments, apparently so out of
      place in the broader movement of the verse? Can you recall
      similar effects in the work of other poets?
(b)   What is happening to the drunk man and what is he seeing?
(c)   Are these pleasant experiences for him?

DISCUSSION

(a)   These passages describe some sort of visionary moment, don't
they? And since they are versions of poems translated from Russian
and German, it seems that the drunk man has experienced
something that other poets have known before him.
(b)   We have been introduced to the drunk man's longing for the
ideal, and this quintessentially Romantic theme runs throughout
the poem as a constant counterpart to its wilder and grosser
extravagances. In fact 'the ideal' is symbolized in many forms in *A
Drunk Man*, but, for the moment, let us remain with her more
traditional manifestion as the muse, the strange 'silken' goddess, or
the mysterious moon.

The 'silken leddy' first appears as a vision of beauty and mystery in the hubbub of a public house. The drunk man senses other realms of being and unsuspected potentiality within himself; and he glimpses something of the ocean depths glittering in her eyes:

> Her gleamin' silks, the taperin'
> O' her ringed fingers, and her feathers
> Move dimly like a dream wi'in,
> While endless faith aboot them gethers.
>
> I seek, in this captivity,
> To pierce the veils that darklin' fa'
> — See white clints slidin' to the sea,   *cliffs*
> And hear the horns o' Elfland blaw.
>
> I ha'e dark secrets turns and twists,
> A sun is gi'en to me to haud,
> The whisky in my bluid insists,
> And speirs my benmaist history, lad.   *asks about; inmost*
>
> And owre my brain the flitterin'
> O' the dim feathers gangs aince mair,
> And, faddomless, the dark blue glitterin'
> O' twa een in the ocean there.

(p.89)

In a moment the vision passes, and it leaves him wondering if it was not a more literal intoxication after all:

> The munelicht's like a lookin'-glass,
> The thistle's like mysel',
> But whaur ye've gane, my bonnie lass,
> Is mair than I can tell.
>
> Were you a vision o' mysel',
> Transmuted by the mellow liquor?
> Neist time I glisk you in a glass,   Next; glimpse
> I'se warrant I'll mak' siccar.   make sure

(p.90)

She may come from the whisky (the one friend always mirrored in his glass), but during the visitation there is no doubt about the poetic power of the experience. Indeed, MacDiarmid's version offers appropriate echoes from Keats's 'Ode to a Nightingale', that other journey to 'the foam of perilous seas, in faery lands forlorn', where the poet is also left wondering 'Was it a vision, or a waking dream?' – 'Is it a dream nae wauk'nin' proves?'

(c)   Are these pleasant experiences then? Well, the second two lyrics will have made it clear that although the hero feels mystery and beauty, he feels terror as well. As a further example of this theme, you should turn to the sequence on p.102 (from 'O wha's the bride that cairries the bunch. . .' to '*My virgin womb ha'e met. . .*'), which evokes the mystery of being and inheritance in the image of a virgin bride who has lain with all men without losing her purity. The magical implications of this, like the stanza form itself, are once more reminiscent of the traditional Scottish ballads, and the style of her speech at the end is certainly in that mode: '*And you sall ha'e my briests like stars, my limbs like willow wands.*' Let us now return to the mainstream of the poem.

'Stream' is the right word in fact, for the poem seems to flow endlessly with no structure apparent beyond its abrupt shifts of mood. MacDiarmid once called it a 'gallimaufry' – a hotch-potch dish full of different ingredients, whose only guiding principle was 'drunkenness' with 'a logic of its own'. Does this satisfy you as a description of the poem? There is some truth in it because, although the poem is an interior journey, it doesn't seem to go anywhere or come to any conclusion.

> Whilst I, puir fule, owre continents unkent   unknown
> And wine-dark oceans waunder like Ulysses
>
> (p.95)

Not surprisingly, then, it repeats itself as it coils and recoils within the intoxicated sensibility of the protagonist. So what *can* we make of it? Can you compare its progress with that of *The Waste Land*, for example – another poem that seems to defy traditional expectations of logic and form?

In fact, its very repetition offers a way of understanding *A Drunk Man's* own peculiar logic, and our discussion of the opening passages has already pointed the way to a critical method. As in *The Waste Land*, it is the recurrence of themes and images which suggests the poem's meaning. In this, *A Drunk Man* is very much a 'modernist' poem, even although its use of monologue and simple rhyme schemes makes it seem more conventional. It is longer, more wildly irregular and sometimes coarser than Eliot's poem. On the other hand, it has a positive energy which the latter lacks. We shall return to this point, but first let us look at those recurring symbols.

The Symbols in 'A Drunk Man'

For the sake of brevity I will deal with the main symbols as follows, in linked, complementary sets:

Thistle: Rose
Woman 'Ideal': Woman 'Real'
Whisky: Moonlight: Sea Serpent

We have already looked at the 'ideal' woman when she appears as
the silken lady and I'll close the discussion of the poem by returning
to her in her 'real' form as Jean, the hero's wife.

As an introduction to the thistle and the rose symbols you should
read the section on pp.119–128 (from 'I saw a rose come loupin'
oot' to '*Shudderin' thistle, gi'e owre, gi'e owre. . .*'). Consider the
following questions as you read, and then go on to the discussion.

Thistle: Rose

(a) Since the 'rose' is the flower on the thistle, what does the
     combination of flower and thorn come to mean to Mac-
     Diarmid?

(b) Do the rose and the silken lady have anything in common?

(c) Does the thistle symbolize Scotland and the Scottish character?
     Or does it refer to a wider condition?

DISCUSSION

(a) Scotland's national plant is supremely ambiguous for Mac-
Diarmid, because it grows both ugly thorns and a bright flower. He
uses this duality to symbolize hope and despair, and these were
both demonstrated for him in the failure of the British General
Strike of May 1926, which he recounts in simple style, rather like a
broadsheet ballad:

I saw a rose come loupin' oot	leaping
Frae a camsteerie plant.	perverse
O wha'd ha'e thocht yon puir stock had	
Sic an inhabitant? . . .	
A rose loupt oot and grew, until	
It was ten times the size	
O' ony rose the thistle afore	
Hed heistit to the skies . . .	hoisted
And still it grew until it seemed	
The haill braid earth had turned	
A reid reid rose that in the lift	sky
Like a ball o' fire burned . . .	

Syne the rose shrivelled suddenly
As a balloon is burst;
The thistle was a ghaistly stick,
As gin it had been curst.   As if

Was it the ancient vicious sway
Imposed itsel' again,
Or nerve owre weak for new emprise
That made the effort vain,

A coward strain in that lorn growth
That wrocht the sorry trick?   wrought
– The thistle like a rocket soared
And cam' doon like the stick.

(pp.119–21)

(b)   We can see that the rose is another form of the ideal that
haunted him in the shape of the silken lady, but in this context the
ideal is a political one. The red flower holds promise of beauty
amidst ugliness, but its spikes make it unapproachable and give
only failure and pain.
(c)   Failure and ugliness seem to the drunk man to be typical of
Scottish culture with its rough-sounding language, its declining
literary tradition and its inheritance of Calvinist grimness:

The language that but sparely flooers
And maistly gangs to weed . . .

(p.122)

Determined to uproot the thistle and to overcome himself, the
drunk man cries '*Yank oot your orra boughs, my hert*' (see pp.115–
17), but this he can never do, for he faces not just a Scottish
dilemma but the universal condition of flawed man. The thistle is
Carlyle's eternal 'nay', everything that frustrates man's hopes, both
from within and without himself. It is the limitation imposed on all
physical beings simply because they *are* physical.

A'thing that ony man can be's
A mockery o' his soul at last.
The mair it shows't the better, and
I'd suner be a tramp than king,
Lest in the pride o' place and poo'er
I e'er forgot my waesomeness.   woefulness
Sae to debauchery and dirt,
And to disease and daith I turn . . .

(p.128)

The final irony is that the ideal rose to which man aspires is an inseparable part of the thistle, bound to its ugliness and pain. Thus the drunk man experiences an endless cycle of attraction and repulsion, hope and despair as he is caught in the puzzle of the flower and its thorns:

> And still the puzzle stands unsolved.
> Beauty and ugliness alike,
> And life and daith and God and man,
> Are aspects o't but nane can tell
> The secret that I'd fain find oot
> O' this bricht hive, this sorry weed,
> The tree that fills the universe,
> Or like a reistit herrin' crines.   dried herring shrivels

(p.126)

In later volumes such as *Stony Limits* and *Second Hymn to Lenin*, MacDiarmid will describe his plight as a longing for 'the impossible song' which is still 'the only song for which I care'. This metaphysical dilemma lies at the heart of his inspiration and, in *A Drunk Man* at least, it leads to a dialectic that is never resolved throughout its length, but only relaxed in the closing lines. Its struggle is enacted again and again – in spiritual anguish and low farce – it is the central topic of the poem and the key to its title, too: *A Drunk Man Looks at the Thistle*.

Whisky: Moonlight: Sea Serpent

We have already noted the inspirational effect of the hero's drunkenness, but in the course of the poem, whisky and moonlight come to symbolize something still more fundamental.

Consider again the opening passages of *A Drunk Man* (from pp.83–98). Notice this time, however, all the references made to whisky and moonlight, and bear the following questions in mind:

(a) What have they in common?
(b) Why have I suggested that they complement each other?
(c) What part do these symbols play in the poem?
(d) What do they come to mean to the hero?
(e) Can you relate them, like the thistle and the rose, to his pursuit of the ideal?

DISCUSSION

Whisky and moonlight do have something in common in the poem
because they both act to transmute reality for the drunk man.
Alcohol excites and confuses his mind and the deceptive, shifting
moonlight makes the landscape seem similarly strange and uncanny.

> Is it the munelicht or a leprosy
> That spreids aboot me, and a thistle
> Or my ain skeleton through wha's bare bones
> A fiendish wund's begood to whistle?. . .   begun
>
> The munelicht ebbs and flows and wi't my thocht,
> Noo' movin' mellow and noo lourd and rough.   heavy

(pp.94, 95)

Thus moonlight and 'moonshine' are associated with each other
and with all the new kinds of knowledge that the hero's experience
brings him:

> That's it! It isna me that's fou at a',   drunk
> But the fu' mune, the doited jade, that's led   full;crazed
> Me fer agley, or 'mogrified the warld . . .   astray

(p.86)

This subjective journey, 'owre continents unkent and wine-dark
oceans', leads him to question the nature of sober 'day-time' reality.

> There's nocht sae sober as a man blin' drunk.
> I maun ha'e got an unco bellyfu'   unusual
> To jaw like this – and yet what I am sayin'
> Is a' the apter, aiblins, to be true.   perhaps
>
> This munelicht's fell like whisky noo I see't   very
> – Am I a thingum mebbe that is kept
> Preserved in spirits in a muckle bottle   big
> Lang centuries efter sin' wi' Jean I slept?
>
> – Mounted on a hillside, wi' the thistles
> And bracken for verisimilitude
> Like a stuffed bird on metal like a brainch,
> Or a seal on a stump o' rock-like wood?
>
> Or am I just a figure in a scene
> O' Scottish life A.D. one-nine-two-five?
> The haill thing kelters like a theatre claith   wavers
> Till I micht fancy that I was alive!

I dinna ken and nae man ever can.   don't know
I micht be in my ain bed efter a'.
The haill damned thing's a dream for ocht we ken,   all that
– The Warld and Life and Daith, Heaven, Hell ana'.   and all

(p.91–2)

The ontological question is pressed home delightfully with the help
of images drawn from the theatre, the pathology lab and the bric-a-
brac of the souvenir trade for tourists in Scotland.

In this way whisky and moonlight transform the drunk man's
usual responses to the world, they loosen his imagination and
promise that complete creative liberation for which he longs.
Nevertheless, his prickly Scottish heritage and an anticipation of his
wife's scorn all too often combine to frustrate him. In other words,
the thistle gets in the way again:

The munelicht is the freedom that I'd ha'e
But for this cursèd Conscience thou hast set in me,

It is morality, the knowledge o' Guid and Ill,
Fear, shame, pity, like a will and wilyart growth.   wrong and wilful
That kills a' else wi'in its reach and craves
Nae less at last than a' the warld to gi'e it scouth.   scope

The need to wark, the need to think, the need to be,
And a' thing that twists Life into a certain shape
And interferes wi' perfect liberty –
These feed this Frankenstein that nae man can escape.

For ilka thing a man can be or think or dae   each
Aye leaves a million mair unbeen, unthocht, undune,
Till his puir warped performance is,
To a' that micht ha' been, a thistle to the mune.

(p.91)

Once again the drunk man's basic dilemma has been stated, as he is
confronted by the thistle – like Blake's Nobodaddy – standing
between him and 'all that might have been'. Yet if awareness itself
and even the 'need to be' is seen as an intolerable burden, is it any
wonder that the protagonist will never find the freedom he desires?
(At least while he is still alive.) Here, indeed, is MacDiarmid's 'True
Scot', 'dominated by the conception of . . . the unattainable'.

Finally, it is the combination of the real effect of whisky and the
symbolical role of the moon that gives the poem much of its
extraordinary fluidity. In these conditions the thistle takes on its
universal aspect and appears to the protagonist in a wild variety of

beautiful and terrible shapes. Thus it becomes a tree, an octopus, a candelabrum, a jellyfish, a dragon, the moon itself, or a whale. I am sure you will already have noticed how these images change in swift succession and interpenetrate as the poem progresses. The unifying symbol of this cosmic puzzle and its endless pursuit is the Sea Serpent.

The 'Sea-Serpent' expresses a central theme whose presence can be discerned in various guises throughout all MacDiarmid's creative life. It first appeared in *Penny Wheep* (p.48), as metaphor for the original and 'only plan' of the universe, long since obscured in the heart of man, and lost even to the recollection of God Himself. At times, however, a poet may be granted a tantalising glimpse of the Serpent's coils:

> Whiles a blindin' movement tak's in my life
> As a quick tide swallows a sea.
> I feel like a star on a starry nicht,
> A'e note in a symphony,
> And ken that the serpent is movin' still,
> A movement that a'thing shares. . .

(*Complete Poems*, p.50)

This creature was later named 'Cencrastus' when it became the controlling symbol of *To Circumjack Cencrastus*, the long poem sequence that followed *A Drunk Man* in 1930. Here the poet set out, once and for all, to 'surround' the elusive beast, which he identified with the 'curly snake' whose spirit inhabits the inter-twining patterns of Celtic art and whose form, with its tail in its mouth, symbolizes eternity. Four years earlier, however, the drunk man had been less ambitious – 'Content to glimpse its loops' without aspiring 'To land the sea serpent's sel' wi' ony gaff' (p.87). Even without the spell of moonlight and whisky, the serpent seems to keep changing its shape, like a protean version of Moby Dick – another symbol of cosmic mystery and terror – which Ahab was compelled to hunt across the oceans of the world. At other times the serpent seems to be within himself, and so, although there may be disgust and anguish at the vision, the drunk man cannot or will not succumb to alienation:

> A mony-brainchin' candelabra fills
> The lift and's lowin' wi' the stars;   blazing
> The Octopus Creation is wallopin'
> In coontless faddoms o' a nameless sea.
> I am the candelabra, and burn
> My endless candles to an Unkent God.

> I am the mind and meanin' o' the octopus
> That thraws its empty airms through a' th' Inane.

(pp.147–8)

If the thistle is 'the puzzle o' man's soul', then the sea serpent is the elusive movement of the cosmos – the 'movement that a 'thing shares'.

Woman: 'real'

Let us close by returning, as the poem does, to the protagonist's wife Jean, and to the part that woman plays in her capacity as a 'real' lover. Read the section from pp.101–115 ('Said my body to my mind. . .' to '. . .be life's licht, my wife!'). Consider the following questions before proceeding to the discussion.
(a)   Does the drunk man present us with a romantic view of love?
(b)   What does his love for Jean mean to him?

DISCUSSION

Well, the drunk man's account of his relationships with real women is egocentric and not exactly respectful, but it tells us a lot about his plight. In fact the act of love with Jean tells him all too much about his physical limitations despite his visions of the ideal. Thus, in the following passage, he wonders if man's spiritual longings can ever be separated from his sexual appetites. Might not one produce the other? In which case, the thistle and all it stands for in the poem may only be the product of sexual frustration? Even if this is not the case, Jean only has to move a leg and all his high-flown longings seem like a child's game:

> I wish I kent the physical basis
> O' a' life's seemin' airs and graces.

It's queer the thochts a kittled cull	tickled testicle
Can lowse or splairgin' glit annul.	set free; splattering sperm
Man's spreit is wi' his ingangs twined	spirit; entrails
In ways that he can ne'er unwind.	
A wumman whiles a bawaw gi'es	scornful look
That clean abaws him gin he sees.	abashes
Or wi' a movement o' a leg	
Shows'm his mind is juist a geg.	token

(p.101)

On the several pages following this passage, the drunk man
explores the physical bond between man and woman and establishes
its importance to a proper and full realization of body and spirit.
MacDiarmid moves through several moods, including Rabelasian
vulgarity and mature and tender understanding, but his philo-
sophical position is not unlike D.H. Lawrence's view that the
intellect is neither balanced nor complete without instinct and the
senses. Compare these two extracts, for example; first with a
prostitute:

> Auld bag o' tricks, ye needna come
> And think to stap me in your womb.   stuff

> You needna fash to rax and strain   trouble to stretch
> Carline, I'll *no* be born again   Hag

> In ony brat you can produce.
> Carline, gi'e owre – O what's the use?

> You pay nae heed but plop me in,
> Syne shove me oot, and winna be din,   done

> – Owre and owre, the same auld trick,
> Cratur withoot climacteric! . . .

(p.109)

And secondly, the drunk man thinks of his wife:

> E'en as the munelicht's borrowed frae the sun
> I ha'e my knowledge o' mysel' frae thee,
> And much that nane but thee can e'er mak' clear,
> Save my licht's frae the source, is dark to me.

> Your acid tongue, vieve lauchter, and hawk's een,   vivid
> And bluid that drobs like hail to quicken me   prickles
> Can turn the mid-day black or midnicht bricht,
> Lowse me frae licht or eke frae darkness free.   Turn me loose

> Bite into me forever mair and lift
> Me clear o' chaos in a great relief
> Till, like this thistle in the munelicht growin',
> I brak in roses owre a hedge o' grief. . . .

(pp.112–13)

If thistle and rose can come together at all, they may be present at
such moments. But the poet's understanding of human love is not
confined to romantic passion alone:

Pit ony couple in a knot
They canna lowse and needna try,   loosen
And mair o' love at last they'll ken
– If ocht! – than joy'll alane descry.   if any

For them as for the beasts, my wife,
A's fer frae dune when pleesure's owre,
And coontless difficulties gar   make
Ilk hert discover a' its power.   Each

I dinna say that bairns alane
Are true love's task – a sairer task
Is aiblins to create oorsels   perhaps
As we can be – it's that I ask . . .

And nae Scot wi' a wumman lies,
But I am he and ken as 'twere
A stage I've passed as he maun pass't,
Gin he grow up, his way wi' her! . . .

He's no' a man ava',   at all
And lacks a proper pride,
Gin less than a' the warld
Can ser' him for a bride! . . .

(pp.113–14)

Thus, even in his love for his wife, the drunk man is haunted by
desire for the rose – for no less than all the world as his bride.

Conclusion

With such high hopes it is no wonder that the seeker exhausts
himself and cries out at times: 'And O! I canna thole / Aye yabblin'
o' my soul, / And fain I wad be free / O' my eternal me'. And no
wonder, in the end, that he comes to Jean for comfort. In his
drunken and visionary state everything has been merging and
changing while psychology, philosophy, history and geography
meet and interpenetrate with extraordinary energy in his mind. At
such pressures, lyrical intensity and raw flippancy collide and
illuminate each other. Fluidity governs all in the poem. There are no
fragments and no ruins in the drunk man's universe, nor is anything
dismissed as irrelevant or unworthy, for in the realm of 'unlimited
possibility', everything has a place. There is no 'Waste Land' on the
drunk man's hillside, but the effort needed to sustain 'fountains
ootloupin' the starns' is prodigious. He feels that he has been
changing shape like Proteus in his pursuit of the changing serpent,
or like Atlas, that he alone has been supporting the whole unsteady

and slippery Creation. In our last passage he recognizes this plight, in a *tour de force* of images and swift shifts from the black and white leaves of Yin and Yang, the eternal Taoist exchange of opposites (or are they liver spots before his drunken eyes?), to the retreat of God into vulgar nationalism. (The extended sequence from which this passage comes is equally brilliant and demanding – it runs from p.128, '*Shudderin' thistle, gi'e owre. . .*', to p.134, 'Thro' bein' mair wudden frae the stert!')

A black leaf owre a white leaf twirls,	
My liver's shadow on my soul,	
And clots o' bluid loup oot frae stems	
That back into the jungle rin,	
Or in the waters underneath	
Kelter like seaweed, while I hear	Waver
Abune the thunder o' the flood,	Above
The voice that aince commanded licht	
Sing 'Scots Wha Ha'e' and hyne awa'	far away
Like Cruivie up a different glen,	
And leave me like a mixture o'	
A wee Scotch nicht and Judgment Day,	
The bile, the Bible, and the *Scotsman*	(Newspaper)
Poetry and pigs – Infernal Thistle,	
Damnation haggis I've spewed up,	
And syne return to like twa dogs!	(Burns's 'The Twa Dogs')
Blin' Proteus wi' leafs or hands	
Or flippers ditherin' in the lift	
– Thou Samson in a warld that has	
Nae pillars but your cheengin' shapes	
That dung doon, rise in ither airts	dashed down; places
Like windblawn reek frae smoo'drin' ess!	smoke from smouldering ash
– Hoo lang maun I gi'e aff your forms	
O' plants and beasts and men and Gods	
And like a doited Atlas bear	crazed
This steeple o' fish, this eemis warld	ill-poised
Or, maniac heid wi' snakes for hair,	
A Maenad, ape Aphrodite,	
And scunner the Eternal sea?	disgust

(p.132)

In the end, the drunk man does not solve his condition – it cannot be solved – nor does he escape it. Nevertheless, he triumphs over it by making it dance to his own tune. If he is finally left with silence, it is not the silence of despair, but the silence of one who has been exhausted and fulfilled simply by the journey itself. It is this, the celebration of man's indomitable spirit, which crowns the poem in

its closing lines: not his visionary ideals, nor death, nor God, but
'him':

> . . . whom nocht in man or Deity,
> Or Daith or Dreid or Laneliness can touch,
> *Wha's deed owre often and has seen owre much.*   died
>
> O I ha'e silence left,
>
>   – 'And weel ye micht',
> Sae Jean'll say, 'eftir sic a nicht!'

(p.167)

A Drunk Man was never intended to be a balanced or a classically
finished poem, for its characteristics are much more clearly in the
modernist vein. Like the endless processes of life itself, it is
dedicated to contradiction, energy and struggle as caught and
mirrored by the leitmotifs of the poet's imagination. Its achievement
is to have 'tried its luck with the idea of chaos' and to have
prevailed with so much passion and good humour.

Part Two
1926–1936

Politics, Science and Philosophical Crisis

Bread from stones is my sole and desperate dearth,
From stones, which are to the Earth as to the sunlight
Is the naked sun which is for no man's sight.
I would scorn to cry to any easier audience. . .

Passage to Whalsay

The publication of *A Drunk Man* might be said to mark the high point of MacDiarmid's early career. Although his first three volumes in Scots had not sold particularly well, they had been praised by discerning readers such as Edwin Muir, 'AE', Compton Mackenzie, Oliver St John Gogarty, Herbert Grierson, Lascelles

"There are plenty of ruined buildings in the world, but no ruined stones." — A Shetland shoreline on the isle of Mousa. The broch in the distance is an ancient Pictish fortified tower. (Photo: Edwin Smith).

Abercrombie and John Buchan. A number of the lyrics were translated into French and Danish, and many others were set to music as the result of the poet's renewed friendship with his former schoolmaster, the composer Francis George Scott, to whom *A Drunk Man* was dedicated. The poet's Montrose years continued to be busy: he started a Scottish centre of the PEN club, and in 1928, as a founder member of the National Party of Scotland, he contested an election in Dundee.[16] MacDiarmid was as sanguine as ever, but there are passages in his next long poem, *To Circumjack Cencrastus*, which express a growing frustration with his job as a not very well-paid journalist in a small town. So when Compton Mackenzie offered him the editorship of *Vox*, – a new magazine on broadcasting – he seized the chance, and towards the end of 1929 he moved to London with his wife and two children.

But things did not go well in the South. A fall from a bus in London gave MacDiarmid serious concussion, and by the time he recovered, *Vox*, always undercapitalized, had perished. His marriage, too, was under strain, and before long Peggy had left him for another man. After various journalistic ventures and some hard drinking, the poet found himself in Liverpool for a short-lived job as public relations officer for Merseyside. *To Circumjack Cencrastus* appeared in 1930, but although it followed in the vein of *A Drunk Man*, it was less successful and the last of his major books in Scots to be accepted by Blackwood's, who had once published James Hogg and Walter Scott.

These depression years were very difficult for MacDiarmid – as for so many others, of course – and on the creative front he felt himself faced with the need to find new expressive themes and means for his verse, including a more overt reflection of his commitment to Socialism. Thus he embarked on the *Hymns to Lenin*, which were to be part of a much larger poetic project of five linked collections conceived as *Clann Albann* ('the children of Scotland'). The first book was to be a set of autobiographical verses called *The Muckle Toon*. The project was never realized, but many of the more personal poems from this period such as 'Kinsfolk', 'At My Father's Grave', 'Charisma and My Relatives' and 'Water of Life', clearly stem from an impulse, perhaps felt for the first time in his life, to reassess his roots at a time of emotional and creative disturbance.

In a number of other poems the rivers of his boyhood were used to symbolize the *élan vital* which he had attributed to Cencrastus, and he was glad to recall that a twisting pathway in the Langfall woods had been known as the 'curly snake'. This perfectly expresses MacDiarmid's conviction that the universal can be found in the particular and that a world of local or private allusion may be made to illuminate the wider human condition. His use of water imagery will make this clearer and a brief digression is in order here.

For MacDiarmid, water is a life *demonstrating* substance rather than a life *giving* one. With this difference in mind, you might care to read 'Water of Life' and 'Excelsior' (*Complete Poems*, pp.314–319), both of which appeared in *First Hymn to Lenin and Other Poems* in 1931. Consider the following questions:

(a) Which qualities in water attract the poet, and what broader issues do they suggest?
(b) Given the title of the collection, do these poems have a political dimension?
(c) Do you recognise any links with *A Drunk Man*, in approach, imagery or theme?

DISCUSSION

(a) It is the sheer mobility of water which excites MacDiarmid:

> Foul here, fair there, to sea and sky again
> The river keeps its course and ranges
>   Unchanged through a' its changes.

(*Complete Poems*, p.316)

This represents the life-enhancing and dangerous evolutionary flux which carries us along and which we ignore or try to dodge at our peril. Such an evolutionary flood is the enemy of comfort and established values, and in 'Excelsior' the poet foresees the possibility of new kinds of existence as far removed from our state today as we already are from the life of eels. You may recall his earlier fancy that the 'Waterside' folk in Langholm were closer to this essential instability because they lived with the danger of floods from the indescribable flux of the river Esk. (Indeed, the long poem 'Water Music' set out to imitate the sounds of this flux in a Joycean linguistic 'babble' of Scots words, each one of which was onomatopoeic and yet descriptively precise, too.)[17]

(b) Although these poems may not be obviously political, they do reflect MacDiarmid's hopes for an evolution towards Socialism and beyond that to a unified life spirit – even if such matters are incomprehensible to the garrulous drinkers in the 'Buck and Croon hotels'. Such changes in perception and behaviour will not be easy, but the shock of 'cauld water' on our preconceptions, or even the threat of extinction itself, may be necessary and salutary stages in 'the strife to tak' new forms'. (MacDiarmid used water as a symbol of the life spirit in his later poems too, most notably in the directly political and yet lyrical expression of 'The Glass of Pure Water' from 1943.)

(c) To return to *A Drunk Man*, we can see that the mobility of water has been carried over from the thistle and the elusive sea serpent, and it is no coincidence that the Gaelic for whisky should be *uisge beatha* – 'water of life'. Furthermore, the poet of 'Water of Life' has felt the 'cant and sweesh' of the primeval flood in the arms of a lover, and this is very reminiscent of what the drunk man discovered between Jean and the silken lady. The reappearance of woman in such a role shows MacDiarmid's debt to (or imprison-ment within) the literary conventions that propose a dominant masculine impulse and a submissive feminine muse; and in this respect, at least, his commitment to change had not yet broken the old Romantic and lyrical moulds. Neverthless, this was soon to happen when he turned to the overtly political and didactic bias of the Hymns to Lenin, and, most notably, when he began to bring scientific materialism into his verse.

Literary conventions apart, the poet's marriage foundered, and he himself had come to depend rather heavily on a less metaphorical 'water of life'. MacDiarmid and Peggy were finally divorced in January 1932. By the end of that year, however, he had married Valda Trevlyn, a Cornish girl met in London, who was to be an invaluable and courageous companion for the rest of his life. The couple moved to a cottage in Sussex from where a limited edition of the *Second Hymn to Lenin* was produced. *Scots Unbound and Other Poems* (1932, another limited edition), was announced as a futher instalment of *Clann Albann*, but an unfavourable review in *The Scots Observer* advised the poet to return to his earlier lyrical style. MacDiarmid repelled the suggestion with a furious letter which resolutely refused to consider the tastes of the Scottish reading public 'in any way'. Even so, he was missing Scotland and, faced with increasing hardship, the couple moved to Edinburgh with their baby son Michael. After further difficulties, MacDiarmid's friends came to his aid and by the summer of 1933, he and his wife and child were established in a low rent cottage near Symbister on Whalsay, one of the Shetland Isles far to the North of Scotland. They were to live there for the next nine years.

In his autobiography MacDiarmid was to recall how he came to Whalsay:

> . . .absolutely down-and-out at the time – with no money behind me
> at all, broken down in health, unable to secure remunerative
> employment of any kind, and wholly concentrated on projects in
> poetry and other literary fields which could bring me no monetary
> return whatsoever. . .[18]

His son recalls the little fisherman's cottage where their first
furniture was made from orange boxes and where they collected
and preserved seagulls' eggs for food.[19] Still, the family gradually
established itself, friends in Edinburgh sent them blankets and
furnishings, and MacDiarmid found publishers and contracts from
prose books such as the essays in *At the Sign of the Thistle* (1934),
and in the same year, a satirical look at Scotland called *Scottish
Scene*, which he shared with the young novelist 'Lewis Grassic
Gibbon' (J. Leslie Mitchell). The biographical sketches of *Scottish
Eccentrics* followed in 1936 and *The Islands of Scotland* (1939),
preceded an enormous autobiography called *Lucky Poet: A Self-
Study in Literature and Political Ideas*, which was eventually
published (in shortened form) in 1943.

The poet was overwhelmed and inspired by the stark grandeur of
the Shetlands, and his letters and essays testify to a fascination with
the striking effects of sea light on bare rock. The austere setting also
made itself felt, as we shall see, in many new poems which are
characterized by their use of geological terms and an icy control in
their English diction. The two major collections from this period,
Stony Limits and Other Poems (1934), and *Second Hymn to Lenin
and Other Poems* from the following year, mark the most
substantial, sustained and innovative conclusion to what I have
called the poet's second period. The 'world language' poems of the
later 1930s and 1940s also date from the Whalsay experience, for
their 'disinterested' and epic scope was confirmed there, and first
published as lengthy extracts in *Lucky Poet*.

The harshness of life on the island, his poor health and the
intense creative pressures of these years all took their toll however,
and MacDiarmid suffered a very serious physical and nervous
breakdown at the end of the summer in 1935. It was seven weeks
before he could leave hospital in Perth and photographs of the time
show him to be emaciated and exhausted even then. Back on
Whalsay he gradually recovered strength, and although he refused
to concede that he was any further from the 'centre of things' than
he had been in Edinburgh or London, it is clear that he did come to
feel increasingly isolated. Having parted from the National Party,
he joined the Communists in 1934 only to be expelled within three

years on account of his nationalism. (He was later reinstated.) As a follower of John Maclean, he saw no contradiction between international Socialism and nationalist hopes for a Scottish workers' republic, but his relationship with any organized political group was never less than stormy. The poem 'Ode to All Rebels' from *Stony Limits* makes his rebel stance entertainingly clear, for he declared perpetual opposition to any system that would shut us off from 'the free, abundant, intolerable licht', and perhaps to all systems whatsoever. His various Nationalist and Socialist positions have been critically discussed in two stimulating essays by Stephen Maxwell and Neal Ascherson.[20]

Determined to remain as uncompromising in his art as he was in his politics, MacDiarmid broke with several old friends, conducting a bitter argument with Edwin Muir, for example, whose pessimistic analysis of Scottish culture, in *Scott and Scotland* (1936), seemed to MacDiarmid a personal betrayal. (Muir's case was that the 'Caledonian antisyzygy' marked a harmful schism rather than creative contradiction, and it deserves fuller consideration than can be given here.) In the same year, a large number of distinguished writers and critics presented MacDiarmid with a public testimonial as a 'creative pioneer' in his services 'to Scots letters and to literature in general'; but when he came to write *Lucky Poet* he could only reflect on how many of them he now regarded as 'mere confounders of counsel and cumberers of the ground, intellectually' (*Lucky Poet*, pp.42–43). Beyond the high spirits and the provocative wit of an autobiography which begins with a warning against letting 'any damned modesty creep in to spoil the story', one can, perhaps, sense MacDiarmid raising his voice a little hectically, in what he felt to be his own, increasingly solitary, space. The creative direction of the third and last phase of his development would not return him to familiar or populated territory.

Poems of Politics and the Spirit

The 'poetry of the thirties' and its prevailing concern with politics is familiar to most readers, not least in the work of MacNeice, Spender, Auden and Day Lewis. English poetry of this period is remarkably cohesive in outlook and style. These young poets felt themselves to be a part of a literary movement with a new social awareness. They published their work, described their aims and kept in touch through the reviews and anthologies produced by writers and editors such as Michael Roberts, Geoffrey Grigson and Kenneth Allott. Socialism had become intellectually respectable in the universities and by the middle of the decade, the Spanish Civil War and the rise of Fascism in Germany and Italy had defined a threat and provided a cause for hundreds of young men and women. Their idealism was to receive many blows in the hard years to come.

It is not surprising, then, that MacDiarmid's poetry of this period should also show an overt concern with socialist issues. Indeed, *First Hymn to Lenin* (1931), was applauded by C. Day Lewis as among the earliest poems of the time to be sympathetic to Communism. Nevertheless, MacDiarmid did not belong with 'MacSpaunday' and company, for his Socialism had radical working-class roots (remember that he joined the ILP when he was sixteen) and as a jobbing journalist for the last twenty years, he did not share the left-wing liberalism or the privileges of a university education. Of the four English poets who were active in 1930, Day Lewis was the eldest at twenty-six and Spender the youngest at twenty-one. They had all studied at Oxford. Day Lewis and Spender worked as critics and editors, Auden earned his living as a schoolmaster and MacNeice was a lecturer in classics. These observations are not intended to belittle the beliefs of the English poets, but they explain why MacDiarmid's 'Socialist' verse often seems closer to propaganda than theirs, and even unbalanced and ugly on occasion. At the same time it makes the almost spiritual aspiration of his later political poems seem all the more remarkable.

It was during the thirties that MacDiarmid began to write more and more in English. He said later that he found Scots unsuitable for conveying his growing interest in matters of science and scientific vocabulary. Furthermore, he had begun to move away from the colloquial informality of address so typical of *A Drunk Man*. In fact this can still be seen in 'The Seamless Garment' and the first two 'Hymns to Lenin'; but when he wrote the 'Third Hymn', 'John Maclean (1879–1923)', 'On a Raised Beach' and many others, he had used English. Nevertheless, his language has a most distinctive character of its own, and to some, it may seem every bit as strange as the Scots of the twenties.

Looking back at many of the 'poems of the thirties' in English literature it is not only their political concerns that strike us, but also their use of then notionally 'unpoetic' material taken from contemporary urban existence. Thus the poets of the period frequently chose images and figures of speech from the city, the factory, or from middle-class culture and furnishings in the home. A fairly representative example would be these lines from Louis MacNeice's 'Birmingham' where he talks of the suburbs:

In these houses men as in a dream pursue the Platonic Forms
With wireless and cairn terriers and gadgets approximating to the
fickle norms
And endeavour to find God and score one over the neighbour
By climbing tentatively upward on jerry-built beauty and sweated
labour.[21]

These lines describe, and hence diagnose, what the poet sees as the sickness of a society where 'Beauty' and 'Truth' have come to mean 'keeping up with the Joneses'. Notice how the verse gains force from the comically overburdened rhythm of the last line and the wicked accuracy with which MacNeice identifies the cairn terrier as the heraldic beast of the middle classes.

Few of MacDiarmid's poems share this mode, and his overtly 'political' pieces tend to the rather grim single-mindedness of a lecture or a sermon instead. He seldom shows the humour or the breadth of satirical observation to be found in the work of his English contemporaries, and the three 'Hymns to Lenin' are a good example of this tendency. You should read them before moving to the more general discussion that follows about political poetry and MacDiarmid's own voice.

DISCUSSION

First of all, we might ask what is meant by 'political poetry'. Is it poetry that advances a consistent doctrine to argue for specific practical behaviour? Or is it poetry written out of a passion that has a political focus? In MacDiarmid's case, and in most cases, I believe that the latter definition is closer to the truth. If we want practical guidance, surely we turn to practical writers? The poets, however, can give us something of the spirit that motivates political ideals and something of the giddy exhilaration that accompanies the prospect of revolutionary action. Such exhilaration is heady stuff and so the poet's role is not necessarily an unimportant one in the world of *realpolitik*. Indeed, it is perhaps the *unspoken* values in the verse that make it all the more seductive and potent because they invoke or imply an attractive community of assent and common purpose – however shadowy or shaky its actual outlines may be. (Consider, for example, the part played by songs in the Spanish Civil War.)

MacDiarmid himself dismissed the role of political theory in his verse by emphasizing that his 'real concern with Socialism is as an artist's organized approach to the interdependencies of life'. (*Lucky Poet*, p.241 n.1). In fact, this understanding of Socialism truly could be said to permeate his creative work, for his imagination was regularly stimulated by just such a perception of complicated interdependencies, as for example in the poems about water already discussed.

However, it must be admitted that many other MacDiarmid poems contain a lot of argument and comparatively little of the concrete 'embodiment' of setting and imagery so tellingly evident in the MacNeice extract. Whether this is a strength or a weakness is what we must now consider. Certainly, it is what distinguishes MacDiarmid's political poetry.

In your reading you will have found that the 'Hymns' value Lenin for what he represents. They seldom expound any actual Leninist doctrine. One of the main things that the poet admires in Lenin is his willingness to embrace extremes for the sake of the ideal. Thus the verses celebrate what often seems to be a heroic ruthlessness, and this may well have disturbing implications. Consider, for example, the closing stanzas from 'First Hymn to Lenin'.

> As necessary, and insignificant, as death
> Wi' a' its agonies in the cosmos still
> The Cheka's* horrors are in their degree;
> And'll end suner! What maitters 't wha we kill
> To lessen that foulest murder that deprives
>   Maist men o' real lives?

> For now in the flower and iron of the truth
> To you we turn; and turn in vain nae mair,
> Ilka fool has folly eneuch for sadness   Every
> But at last we are wise and wi' laughter tear
> The veil of being, and are face to face
>   Wi' the human race.

> Here lies your secret, O Lenin, – yours and oors,
> No' in the majority will that accepts the result
> But in the real will that bides its time . . .

(*Complete Poems*, p.298)
* Founded in 1917 to combat counter-revolution and sabotage.

How do you feel about that undoubtedly stirring antithesis – 'the flower and iron of the truth'? I am moved by its revolutionary toughness, but I am also bothered by the poet's apology for the secret police, the Cheka, and his question 'What does it matter who we kill?' (It would seem that Stalin wanted to share some of that toughness, for his adopted name means 'man of steel'.) To give MacDiarmid credit, he does choose to name the Cheka in the first place, and so we cannot accuse him of trying to hide things from us.

But in mentioning it at all, I feel that he loses the assent of his readers. He loses mine, anyway, even when allowances are made for the advantage of hindsight.

By way of comparison, consider this much shorter poem from *Stony Limits* in 1934:

The Skeleton of the Future

At Lenin's Tomb

Red granite and black diorite, with the blue
Of the labradorite crystals gleaming like precious stones
In the light reflected from the snow; and behind them
The eternal lightning of Lenin's bones.

(*Complete Poems*, p.386)

This is very succinct yet still says a great deal, especially through its use of geological vocabulary. What would you say this does for it?

DISCUSSION

The geological terms evoke an unyielding, crystalline and brilliant hardness. The spirit of Lenin is symbolized by cold light from snow, and his message burns like a dangerous electric storm in the very bones of the corpse preserved in its tomb. The poem, like its title, manages to convey a glittering menace, and, at the same time, it excites us with its sternness. These four lines say a great deal to me about the intellectual challenge of Dialectical Materialism and the delights and dangers of its discipline. I understand what Leninism means to MacDiarmid when I read the poem and I accede to the 'flower and iron' of its fascination. (Perhaps the 'Northern' environment and a fierce history of Presbyterian dispute have made the Scottish psyche particularly responsive to such effects.) But the attempt to *argue* much the same case in the 'First Hymn' fails to convince me. If you follow this point (whether you agree with it or not) you may care to consider what it tells of our assumptions about the nature of poetry and the susceptibility of the reader. The second poem convinces me more by saying less. Iain Crichton Smith makes a similar point about the 'statements' of 'On a Raised Beach', as opposed to the lyricism he admires in 'The Eemis Stane'. In that example I don't agree with him, but you should consider his essay for yourselves.[22]

The 'Second Hymn to Lenin' appeared in 1932, and it continues the style of argument seen in its predecessor. Let us return to it with the following question in mind. Is this poem about MacDiarmid's hopes for politics or his hopes for poetry?

DISCUSSION

In a sense, the answer to our question is 'neither', for the poet
makes it clear that he regards both politics and poetry only as the
means to a further end, which is to develop man's spirit and come
'face to face wi' the human race'. But of the two, his understanding
of 'poetry' would *include* 'politics' on the way to this ultimate goal:

> Sae here, twixt poetry and politics,
> There's nae doot in the en'.
> Poetry includes that and s'ud be
> The greatest poo'er amang men.

(*Complete Poems*, p.326)

Material problems are important, but MacDiarmid regards them as
the easiest of tasks and he is impatient that they should still be
unresolved.

> *Oh, it's nonsense, nonsense, nonsense,*
> *Nonsense at this time o' day*
> *That breid-and-butter problems*
> *S'ud be in ony man's way.*

> *They s'ud be like the tails we tint*   lost
> *On leavin' the monkey stage,*
> *A' maist folk fash aboot's alike*   vex themselves about
> *Primaeval to oor age.*

> *We're grown-ups that haena yet*
> *Put bairnly things aside*
> *– A' that's material and moral –*
> *And oor new state descried.*

> *Sport, love, and parentage,*
> *Trade, politics, and law*
> *S'ud be nae mair to us than braith*
> *We hardly ken we draw.*

> *Freein' oor poo'ers for greater things,*
> *And fegs there's a plenty o' them,*   And faith
> *Tho' wha's still trammelt in alow*   trampled down
> *Canna be tenty o' them –*   Cannot be mindful

(p.325)

In the context of 'greater things' his hopes for an important role for
poetry seem admirable. Yet he must also face the fact that most
people don't read verse:

> *Are my poems spoken in the factories and fields,*
> *In the streets o' the toon?*
> *Gin they're no', then I'm failin' to dae*
> *What I ocht to ha' dune.*

(p.323)

He raises the question, but cannot resolve it. If it is taken at its most literal level, then I am not sure that any great artist has resolved it. In the meantime, the poet searches for the elusive principle of organization that will allow him to mobilize his powers as effectively as Lenin structured his political insight.

> Unremittin', relentless,
> Organized to the last degree,
> Ah, Lenin, politics is bairns' play
> To what this maun be!   must be

(p.328)

Once again I think that MacDiarmid's argument fails to convince me, precisely because he makes it an argument rather than a poem. Do you agree with this view? (I do like individual passages, however, such as the sequence '*Oh, it's nonsense, nonsense. . .*') The danger of choosing a style of reasoned debate for one's work is that poetry may have more to do with quality of expression than it has to do with content. Even the best case will not make a poem. Therefore I am critical of some of the weaknesses in the 'Second Hymn'. Here is a stanza, for example, which seems to me to operate at a very low pressure indeed – and not only because it paraphrases the Bible via Wordsworth!

> You confined yoursel' to your work
> – A step at a time;
> But, as the loon is in the man,   boy
> That'll be ta'en up i' the rhyme.

(p.326)

My objection can be countered by pointing out that MacDiarmid *wanted* his verse to have a certain plainness, and that my understanding of 'poetry' and 'quality of expression' derives from lyrical, post-Romantic and bourgeois assumptions about literature. This may be so, but I'm still not persuaded that the stanza is poetry, and I would rally by noting that MacDiarmid's own claims for 'the poet' and his messianic social or creative role, display all the values of a 'high art' tradition. (It is one of the paradoxes of his Socialist position that, despite his use of vernacular Scots, MacDiarmid had no time for oral and folk culture.)

These issues are examined further by David Craig – himself a Marxist critic – in his essay 'MacDiarmid the Marxist Poet'.[23] One of the poems he particularly admires is 'Lo! A Child is Born' (1935), which he calls an allegory of the birth pangs of history:

Lo! A Child is Born

I thought of a house where the stones seemed suddenly changed
And became instinct with hope, hope as solid as themselves,
And the atmosphere warm with that lovely heat,
The warmth of tenderness and longing souls, the smiling anxiety
That rules a home where a child is about to be born.
The walls were full of ears. All voices were lowered.
Only the mother had the right to groan or complain.
Then I thought of the whole world. Who cares for its travail
And seeks to encompass it in like lovingkindness and peace?
There is a monstrous din of the sterile who contribute nothing
To the great end in view, and the future fumbles,
A bad birth, not like the child in that gracious home
Heard in the quietness turning in its mother's womb,
A strategic mind already, seeking the best way
To present himself to life, and at last, resolved,
Springing into history quivering like a fish,
Dropping into the world like a ripe fruit in due time. –
But where is the Past to which Time, smiling through her tears
At her new-born son, can turn crying: 'I love you'?

(p.548)

DISCUSSION

Here is what Craig has to say about the poem's conclusion:

The peak of intensity is reached in the splendid double simile of fish and fruit. Here feelings are marvellously united: the measured, nearly Biblical gravity of the repeated participles, 'Springing. . . Dropping', allied to the richness of the images, creates a feeling both springy and solid. The momentum at this point seems to flow onwards and yet gathers itself monumentally. With the unerring touch of genius the poet has evoked sheer vitality in nature and at the same time the experience of dwelling on it with steady intellectual intent.
　　The lines remind me strongly of Yeats's consummate passage from 'Sailing to Byzantium':

> . . .The young
> In one another's arms, birds in the trees
> – Those dying generations – at their song. . .

Craig concludes that, although it is less clearly Socialist than other poems of the period, 'Lo! A Child is Born' still draws directly from MacDiarmid's Marxism in its sense of 'the whole of humanity's historic struggle to develop'.

I agree with these comments[24], but I also feel as I did with 'The Skeleton of the Future', that this poem convinces me because it operates through metaphor, and not by didactic debate. That, at least, is the view I have taken so far, but the next question is – need this *always* be the case? To help answer this, let us turn to 'The Seamless Garment' (*Complete Poems*, pp.311–14).

I would suggest that 'The Seamless Garment' (from the *First Hymn* collection) is MacDiarmid's most successfully didactic poem because it achieves a unity of content and style that escapes the 'Second Hymn' and because it attempts to persuade without arousing hate in us. The very title, 'The Seamless Garment' suggests an ideal of wholeness and unity. In fact the reference is to a garment of Christ's for which the Roman soldiers cast lots at the foot of the cross. According to John, 19:23, this was 'a coat without seam, woven from the top throughout'. In the accretions of medieval theology, however, this humble coat came to represent the purity of the Saviour, and its 'seamlessness' became a symbol of his life. Despite these hints at a spiritual ideal, the verse is written in everyday colloquial Scots whose plainness manages to be effective without being condescending when it offers advice to a 'cousin' in a Langholm woollen mill.

You should now read the poem before tackling the discussion with the following questions in mind:
(a)   In what way is this a political poem, and, indeed, is it one at all?
(b)   What are the qualities that MacDiarmid finds in the mill and admires among the workers?
(c)   What is the central symbol of the poem, and does it convince us?

DISCUSSION

(a)   MacDiarmid suggests that Lenin had a vision of a single reality behind the infinite variety of human strife and he adds that a great poet such as Rilke had it too. Thus, once again, it is not a specific political doctrine of Lenin's that the poet celebrates, but a quality *demonstrated* by him. In the same way, the weaver is at home in a mill which is an intricate and meaningful whole to him, but only noise and confusion to the newcomer. To weave the seamless garment is to pursue this whole and to achieve a complete fusion between life and work, belief and action.

> What's life or God or what you may ca't
>> But something at ane like this?

(p.312)

I find this politically effective because of its assurance that such unity is the birthright of everyone and that, although it begins on the factory floor, it need not end there.
(b)   The poet admires the weaver because his skill at the loom and his understanding of the mill is a marvel of unforced constructive action:

> The womenfolk ken what I mean.
>> Things maun fit like a glove,   must
> Come clean off the spoon – and syne   then
>> There's time for life and love.

(p.313)

And MacDiarmid asks his friend to apply these abilities beyond his work, to himself, his life and his fellow men, otherwise, 'Mony a loom mair alive than the weaver seems':

> The mair we mak' natural as breathin' the mair
> Energy for ither things we'll can spare,
>> But as lang as we bide like this   remain
> Neist to naething we ha'e, or miss.

(p.313)

Here, as in the 'Second Hymn', we glimpse MacDiarmid's impatience with the merely material problems that still afflict us, when the greater challenge is to bring about a change in man's nature itself. Politics is only one step towards the seamless integrity that so fascinates him, even although we may never attain it – 'the sun's still nearer than Rilke's dreams'.
(c)   Finally, the symbols of mill and cloth are good ones. The multiplicity of forces, tensions and mechanical activities of the mill all go towards the one fabric and its creation from thousands of single threads. In the end, MacDiarmid wants this coherence for his own work, too, and the poem closes by bringing both poetry and politics to a single conclusion:

I ken fu' weel
Sic an integrity's what I maun ha'e
   Indivisible, real,
Woven owre close for the point o' a pin   too
   Onywhere to win in.

(p.314)

I think that 'The Seamless Garment' is one of the very few of
MacDiarmid's overtly political pieces to combine successfully both
polemic and poetry. The verse progresses by a calm and unhurriedly
reasonable argument – in the manner of the 'Second Hymn', if you
like – but it also contains the metaphorical subtlety of 'Lo! A Child
is Born'. You may feel that it is not entirely free from the kind of
slack rhyme that I pointed out in the 'Second Hymn'. Consider this
notable example.

   Is't no' high time
We were tryin' to come into line a' roon?
   (I canna think o' a rhyme.)
Machinery in a week mak's greater advances
Than Man's nature twixt Adam and this.

(p.313)

Does the poet get away with it? In this case I think that he does,
although you may not agree. I would defend him by claiming that
the poem does purport to be a conversation between the writer and
his cousin. So this aside, with its wry confession of failure,
reinforces the informality of the occasion, and protects him from
the accusation that he is a 'highbrow' preaching to the workers. If
you still feel worried by it, you could reply to my case by suggesting
that the passage is a little self-conscious and perilously close to the
'simple rhymes for silly folk' that MacDiarmid scorned in the
'Second Hymn'. I can only answer this by referring to the poem's
overall tone, by which, for me at least, 'The Seamless Garment'
remains simple, and simply effective, without being ingenuous.

   I suggested earlier that MacDiarmid was more of a Marxian
idealist than a social commentor, even in his 'political' poems.
Indeed, the condition of unity in complexity which he sees in the
symbolic 'seamless garment', is very similar to the goal that had
been so passionately sought by the drunk man in all its various
manifestations as rose, silken lady or sea serpent. However, there is
one important difference in the poet's position, for the drunk man
was an essentially Romantic figure who pursued the twists and
turns of his *own* sensibility, and met it reflected again throughout

the world. If the MacDiarmid of the thirties does uphold the same ideal, then he no longer seeks for it so certainly within, or through, himself. Hence the more outward-looking stance taken by all the political poems discussed so far. Furthermore, his Marxist materialism and a growing interest in scientific vocabularies led him to refer more and more to the possibility of 'an *organized* approach to the interdependencies of life'. In *A Drunk Man*, on the other hand, he had attempted to embrace life through its *unorganized* contradictions.

MacDiarmid's fascination with work that was to be 'Unremitting, relentless, organized to the last degree', continued to grow throughout the thirties, and it led to those enormous catalogues of the material world that he built into the 'epic' poems of his 'third period'. The impulse remained the same, but the means towards its attainment had changed. One could characterize this change by saying that what had been, in the twenties, an exhilarating (and largely psychological), celebration of chaos had become, by the forties, an elaborate inventory of different kinds of arcane and complex information. A key poem whose style bridges this development is 'In the Slums of Glasgow'.

Nowhere in MacDiarmid's work is the 'seamless garment' more clearly recognized as a perception of life's fundamental unity than in 'In the Slums of Glasgow', published in 1935 in *Second Hymn to Lenin and Other Poems*. Read the poem (*Complete Poems*, pp.562–65) and bear in mind these questions.

(a)   Given the title, is this a poem of social, satirical or political comment?

(b)   What is the prevailing attitude adopted by the poet?

(c)   Consider its structure and diction, and how MacDiarmid makes his case forceful. How would you describe his English?

DISCUSSION

(a)   As far as the first question goes, it seems that the 'furniture' of MacDiarmid's poem is overtly religious and philosophical, rather than political. He refers to Hindu mysticism, to the Greek philosopher Thales (who speculated that water was the fundamental substance of the universe), to Boethius and to Christianity. Of course, MacDiarmid's setting is in the slums but what he is writing about is not confined there – it is 'abundant in the slums as everywhere else' and he revolts against the idea of judging these oppressed people as 'the despised slum crowd'.

(b)   What attitude does the poet take? MacDiarmid's tone is one of spiritual revelation, and his focus is less social than metaphysical:

> The same earth produces diamonds, rock-crystal, and vermilion,
> The same sun produces all sorts of plants, the same food
> Is converted into hair, nails and many other forms.
> These dogmas are not as I once thought true nor as afterwards false
> But each the empty shadow of an intimate personal mood.
> I am indifferent to shadows, possessing the substance now.
> I too look on the world and behold it is good.

(p.562)

Here is all the optimism of *A Drunk Man*, and more. Describing no less than a visionary experience, MacDiarmid uses terms drawn from scientific materialism. It is an astonishing mixture. And, once again, he compares life to water, which retains its fundamental unity however often the outward form may change.

> I am deluded by appearances no more – I have seen
> The goodness, passion and darkness from which all things spring,
> Identical and abundant in the slums as everywhere else . . .
>
> Foam, waves, billows and bubbles are not different from the sea,
> But riding the bright heavens or to the dark roots of earth sinking
> Water is multiform, indivisible and one,
> Not to be confused with any of the shapes it is taking.

(p.563)

(c)   This brings us to the structure and diction of 'In the Slums of Glasgow'. MacDiarmid's English is polysyllabic, Latinate in its vocabulary, and it uses abstract scientific terminology to describe an even more abstracted visionary moment. The result is an elevated diction, which gains considerable emphasis from its use of long lines, extended sentences and a single linking rhyme in every second line of each section, (*ab cb db eb fb gb*, etc.). The effect is one of complexity, and yet the lines flow inexorably towards a single conclusion. In other words, the style acts out the perception it describes.

Consider, for example, the following passage, which makes one sentence, and note, too, what its meaning is:

> All opposing psychic tendencies are resolved in sweet song
> My eyes discard all idle shows and dwell instead
> In my intercourse with every man and woman I know
> On the openings and shuttings of eyes, the motions of mind, and,
>   especially, life, and are led
> Beyond colour, savour, odour, tangibility, numbers, extensions,

Individuality, conjunction, disjunction, priority, posterity – like an
    arrow sped,
And sheer through intellection, volition, desire, aversion,
Pleasure, pain, merit and demerit – to the fountain-head,
To the unproduced, unproducing, solitary, motionless soul
By which alone they can be known, by which alone we are not
    misled.

(p.563)

This is an extraordinary diction. MacDiarmid has become a sort of
Milton, or, more appropriately, a Carlyle whose radical didacticism
has been fired by Biblical language and the Prebyterian tradition of
the learned sermon. The intimate and concrete effects of the short
Scots lyrics seem very far away indeed. Yet the passage has an
undeniable rhetorical power. Furthermore, the fascination with
language, which bore such fruit in the Scots poems, is still there.
And we can still find MacDiarmid's delight in unexpected
combinations, as when 'psychic tendencies' are linked with 'sweet
song'; and when that lengthy recital of abstract qualities leads us to
the romanticism of 'fountain-head' and 'motionless soul'.

Finally, let us consider how the poem closes. In fact it fades away
into an onomatopoeic version of the city's noise. The poet's
attention leaves the radiant abstractions of his discourse and comes
to rest on the single and intimate detail of his lover's eyelashes
touching his cheek. After so long at such 'high altitudes' it is a
startlingly effective transition, and it suggests that MacDiarmid
knows exactly what he is doing in this rhetorical mode. Even the
receding noises might be said to begin with hints of the negative –
'Na nonanunno', and to end with similar variations on the
affirmative – 'Dadado' etc.

What are we to make of 'In the Slums of Glasgow'? It is certainly
not about politics and living conditions, and yet I believe that its
vision is at the heart of the poet's concern with social equality. Like
Blake, he celebrates 'the glad wells of being' and upholds the
unfettered expansion of every person's spirit:

The sin against the Holy Ghost is to fetter or clog
The free impulse of life. . .

(p.564)

There is nothing quite like this poem in English writing of the
period. It makes a unique and sometimes strange blend of polemic
and vision, expressed with a powerful and unselfconscious rhetoric.
Whereas a sophisticated irony seems to temper many of the poems

of the thirties' writers, it is a quality completely lacking in MacDiarmid. Some critics would claim that irony is inevitably found in modern literature, because it recognizes – wryly enough – that the individual can no longer hope for a heroic role in our contemporary world. Others might see it as a special kind of defeatism. Does MacDiarmid's lack of irony weaken or strengthen the credibility of his poems? Does the rhetoric seem excessive? Or are you carried along, only to wonder if you have been tricked at the end? There are no easy answers to these questions, but they offer themselves for further debate and, I hope, lively disagreements.

A Poetry of Thought

I want to close this section of MacDiarmid's work and life by considering 'On a Raised Beach', a long philosophical meditation, and one of his most remarkable poems.[25]

Beyond question, 'On a Raised Beach' is related to the personal crisis that MacDiarmid underwent in the mid-1930s and its searchingly existential focus found the perfect correlative in the severe and nothern landscape of Whalsay among the Shetland Isles. The Shetlands are like nowhere else in Britain, and to a stranger they may seem at first to be bleak and desolate. Here is MacDiarmid's description of what he found there:

> It may take [visitors] a little time to realize that what is affecting them is the total absence of trees and of running water. But . . . we soon realize that their absence throws into relief features we seldom see or underprize because of them – the infinite beauties of the bare land and the shapes and colours of the rocks . . .
>
> It is in fact the treasures and rich lessons of a certain asceticism the Shetlands provide . . . The lack of ostentatious appearances, the seeming bareness and reserve, make the Shetlands insusceptible of being readily or quickly understood; one must steep oneself in them, let them grow upon one, to savour them properly. It is a splendid discipline.[26]

This passage does much to explain the austerity of the poem and its search for that 'splendid discipline'. MacDiarmid's Socialist idealism, his admiration of Lenin, his growing interest in scientific materialism, and the remoteness of Shetland, all these come together to inform the spirit of the piece.

> It is a frenzied and chaotic age,
> Like a growth of weeds on the site of a demolished building.
> How shall we set ourselves against it,
> Imperturbable, inscrutable, in the world and yet not in it . . .

By what immense exercise of will,
Inconceivable discipline, courage, and endurance,
Self-purification and anti-humanity,
Be ourselves without interruption,
Adamantine and inexorable?

(*Complete Poems*, p.429)

In geology a 'raised beach' is a beach beyond the high tide mark, or well above it or even far inland from the sea. In other words, it dates from when the contours of the world were different. On such a beach and from this perspective the poet contemplates the nature of reality and the human spirit. He finds courage in this setting and it is as though he has escaped from human passions and weaknesses to find peace in an almost terrifying vision of bareness, endurance and endless time.

In the stones around him, the poet finds a parable of life reduced to the minimum, and in a single rock he confronts no less than the absolute indifference of all the created world.

What happens to us
Is irrelevant to the world's geology
But what happens to the world's geology
Is not irrelevant to us.

(p.428)

Yet the poem offers a most strikingly intense insight into the 'thisness' of the stones, and in them the poet finds the condition he seems to desire for himself – a cold, clear, ageless, passionless and inscrutable unity:

Here a man must shed the encumbrances that muffle
Contact with elemental things, the subtleties
That seem inseparable from a humane life, and go apart
Into a simpler and sterner, more beautiful and more oppressive world,
Austerely intoxicating; the first draught is overpowering;
Few survive it.

(p.428)

If these lines seem inhuman and even very much like a contemplation of suicide, then MacDiarmid recognizes this but still insists that a better life can only be built by starting from such fundamentals, otherwise, 'we have not built on rock'.

Death is a physical horror to me no more.
I am prepared with everything else to share
Sunshine and darkness and wind and rain
And life and death bare as these rocks though it be. . .

(p.428)

If *A Drunk Man* saw the poet grappling with the energy and chaos of the universe as reflected in his own overheated mind, then 'On a Raised Beach' shows him confronting the terrible and static disinterestedness of the physical world as a place entirely apart from any merely human concerns. Yet still, as before, his achievement is to find a place for the human spirit. A similar confrontation lies at the heart of the drama of the absurd and it is particularly present in the work of Samuel Beckett. You may care to reflect on this as you read the poem and then the discussion below. Here are the questions I will raise:

(a)   What can we make of the style? For example, what kind of sense do you make of the opening lines?
(b)   What do the stones symbolize?
(c)   Does the poem have a political aspect?
(d)   Is its vision grim or uplifting?

DISCUSSION

(a)   The first thing to strike a reader must be the vocabulary with which the poem opens and closes. MacDiarmid draws his words from geology, architecture, and the most abstruse and learned recesses of the dictionary. A rough 'translation' of the opening lines (pp. 422–3) would go as follows:

> All is born out of stones – or is discharged after-birth,
> Fossil fruit of the forbidden tree, [in Eden]
> Stones blacker than any in the sacred shrine at Mecca,
> Cream-coloured like the building-stone in Normandy, or lustrous
> pieces [changeable as in a cat's eye],
> Willow-green and dark green-to-black, dark sooty-brown and beige,
> With a green-grey bloom, frosted, black as a thundercloud, cup-
> shaped,
> Making mere bright-spots [as on the surface of the sun] of the sun
> and moon,
> I study you sulky and gleaming, but have
> No gem-lathe to adjust you with, and turn again
> From seeing to feeling and like a blind man run
> My fingers over you, cutting edge by edge, burr by burr,
> Smooth-surfaced mineral planes, trout-speckles, wrinkles, pitted
> holes,
> Bringing my sense perceptions in vain to bear,
> A tiny angle to all your corrugations and projecting corners,
> Cross-engraved, perforated, sunken-carved-relief of the world,
> Directly expository, dependable stones, thousand-year-era by era
> What ancient military catapult piled you here, stupendous cairn?
> What artist poses the earth flayed-open for anatomical study thus,
> Pillar of creation heraldically-deviced in me?

What process of becoming-hard like ivory augments you with men's
        bones,
Every fanatic devotee still a beautiful youth asleep in dreams?
        [loved by the moon-goddess as in the Classical myth]
All the other stones are in this inexpressible 'thisness' it seems,
But where is the Christ-manifesting rock that moved? [from the
        tomb in Gethsemane]
What song from the mystic gods of the ancient classical world comes
        from this block where slaves are auctioned?

So the introduction does make sense, after all. But surely it asks too
much of us – or of any reader's patience with the dictionary[27] The
question is, does the passage serve a more immediate purpose, even
before it has been 'decoded'? Look at it again.

It seems to me to be as much dramatic as informative, and
MacDiarmid's aim is to conjure up the strange and resistant world
of stones with what amounts to a magical incantation. Equally, it
might be seen as the invocation to the muse which is traditionally
made at the beginning of epic verse. And then again, in a modernist
context, it serves to shake up our comfortable assumptions about
language, which is itself 'made strange' and shown in a new and
disturbing light. This last point is made clearer by the next lines,
which drop into a sudden, startling clarity to explain that:

Deep conviction or preference can seldom
Find direct terms in which to express itself.
To-day on this shingle shelf
I understand this pensive reluctance so well,
This is not discommendable obstinacy

(p.423)

In fact, a 'pensive reluctance' characterizes the style of the whole
poem. The diction is Latinate, highly intellectual and its long lines
give a sense of great weight being brought to bear – 'without
interruption, adamantine and inexorable' – indeed. If the lines are
slow-moving and sometimes awkward, they still suit the harsh
world the poet is attempting to approach, a world where all else is
stripped bare and where he himself, seems to turn to stone:

Impatience is a poor qualification for immortality.
Hot blood is of no use in dealing with eternity.
It is seldom that promises or even realisations
Can sustain a clear and searching gaze.
But an emotion chilled is an emotion controlled;
This is the road leading to certainty. . .

(pp.425–6)

This voice is already familiar from 'In the Slums of Glasgow'. MacDiarmid came to use it increasingly, and some of his later poems are over-burdened with its polysyllabic and portentous manner. 'On a Raised Beach', however, seems to be a brilliantly successful and unified poem in this mode, and his most original contribution to style in modern English poetry. T.S. Eliot solved the problem of writing a long meditative poem by using a different style in each section of each of his *Quartets*, but 'On a Raised Beach' does not adopt this variety. It sustains instead a single and powerful note throughout its course: not so much a quartet as a pibroch – that stern and unrelentingly classical music of the bagpipes.

(b)   What do the stones symbolize? To answer this we might begin by considering the way Eliot writes about stones in *The Waste Land* and 'The Hollow Men'. One difference is immediately apparent, the stones are images of sterility and ruin for Eliot but not for MacDiarmid:

> We must be humble. We are so easily baffled by appearances
> And do not realise that these stones are one with the stars.
> It makes no difference to them whether they are high or low,
> Mountain peak or ocean floor, palace, or pigsty.
> There are plenty of ruined buildings in the world but no ruined
>   stones.
> No visitor comes from the stars
> But is the same as they are.

  (p.425)

The theme is the now familiar one of the unity of all creation, but it is a reductive and severe unity, not a sentimental tolerance of everything:

> This is no heap of broken images.
> Let men find the faith that builds mountains
> Before they seek the faith that moves them. Men cannot hope
> To survive the fall of the mountains
> Which they will no more see than they saw their rise
> Unless they are more concentrated and determined,
> Truer to themselves and with more to be true to,
> Than these stones, and as inerrable as they are.
> Their sole concern is that what can be shaken
> Shall be shaken and disappear
> And only the unshakable be left.

  (p.427)

These last lines are an echo of the creative destruction advocated by the nineteenth-century Russian Nihilist, Dmitry Pisarev – 'What

can be smashed should be smashed. With withstands the blow is fit
to survive'. Pisarev was a champion of the individual against the
authority of State or tradition, and indeed his words do have
a revolutionary ardour in the line with MacDiarmid's occasional
admiration for ruthless action, (much more stridently expressed,
for example, in the 'Third Hymn to Lenin').

Is there an implied criticism of religion in such passages from 'On
a Raised Beach'? I think that there is. MacDiarmid comes directly
and sternly to the stones and to the materialistic truth they
represent for him. He has no time for the rituals of mass and prayer,
or for religion as consolation, as witness the multiple puns on the
geological term 'crusta', and on the seas as 'bead proof', which I
take to mean both alcoholic and proof against the comfort of the
rosary.

> Do not argue with me. Argue with these stones.
> Truth has no trouble in knowing itself.
> This is it. The hard fact. The inoppugnable reality,
> Here is something for you to digest.
> Eat this and we'll see what appetite you have left
> For a world hereafter.
> I pledge you in the first and last crusta,
> The rocks rattling in the bead-proof seas.

> (p.430)

He may not be writing in Scots but there is no mistaking the
Scottish Calvinist heritage in these lines, with their delight in a
rock-hard accommodation to discipline. Thomas Carlyle's essay on
'The Hero as Priest' expressed just the same grim Scottish approval
of John Knox's commitment to reality as he saw it, as if he were
some 'Old-Hebrew Prophet' with 'the same inflexibility, intolerance,
rigid narrow-looking adherence to God's truth, stern rebuke . . . to
all that forsake truth. . .' MacDiarmid may claim to be an atheist,
but his certainty has a truly Knoxian ring to it – 'Listen to me', he
writes:

> . . . – Truth is not crushed;
> It crushes, gorgonises all else into itself.
> The trouble is to know it when you see it?
> You will have no trouble with it when you do.

> (p.430)

There is a line in Burns's work that sums up this very Northern
outlook like a proverb – 'facts are cheels that winna ding' – facts
are fellows who won't be overcome, facts cannot be got round,
however much we would like it otherwise:

> 'Ah!' you say, 'if only one of these stones would move
> – Were it only an inch – of its own accord
>   This is the resurrection we await,
> – The stone rolled away from the tomb of the Lord.

(p.432)

But the poet will have nothing of the faith that 'moves mountains';
nor does he hold out much hope for charity:

> (The masses too have begged bread from stones,
> From human stones, including themselves,
> And only got it, not from their fellow-men,
> But from stones such as these here – if then.)
> Detached intellectuals, not one stone will move,
> Not the least of them, not a fraction of an inch. . .

(p.432)

(c) Very well then, you may say, if it rejects religion, does 'On a
Raised Beach' offer materialism instead? Is it, indeed, a political
poem? Consider, for example, its forceful insistence on the absolute
physicality of the world and on the discipline necessary for those
who would change it:

> It will be ever increasingly necessary to find
> In the interests of all mankind
> Men capable of rejecting all that all other men
>   Think, as a stone remains
> Essential to the world, inseparable from it,
>   And rejects all other life yet.
> Great work cannot be combined with surrender to the crowd.

(p.429)

This has something of the hardness that marked the poet's hopes in
'Second Hymn to Lenin' – 'unremittin', relentless, / Organized to
the last degree'. At the close of '. . .Raised Beach' he comes to
address 'detached intellectuals' by advising them to get down to the
'ground bass' he has been following:

>   . . . It is not
> The reality of life that is hard to know.
> It is nearest of all and easiest to grasp,
> But you must participate in it to proclaim it.

(p.432)

But, we might ask, participate in what, and how? Or is this only a
gesture towards social 'commitment' and orthodox Marxism? In

fact, the next lines tell us that the poet is not suggesting a social programme only, but something a good deal more fundamental:

> – I lift a stone; it is the meaning of life I clasp
> Which is death, for that is the meaning of death;
> How else does any man yet participate
>   In the life of a stone,
> How else can any man yet become
> Sufficiently at one with creation, sufficiently alone,
> Till as the stone that covers him he lies dumb
> And the stone at the mouth of his grave is not overthrown?

(pp.432–3)

To approach the condition of stone, completely alone, silent and at one with creation, is, indeed, to come close to death. He meditates on this supreme isolation and wonders if he has the strength and the singleness of purpose and the 'Spartan impassivity' to survive. 'These stones have the silence of supreme creative power':

> It is not a question of escaping from life
> But the reverse – a question of acquiring the power
> To exercise the loneliness, the independence, of stones,
> And that only comes from knowing that our function remains
> However isolated we seem fundamental to life as theirs.
>   We have lost the grounds of our being,
>   We have not built on rock.

(p.431)

It is this search for 'rock' that MacDiarmid feels must precede all human activity, whether it is artistic, or political. As with 'In the Slums of Glasgow', his aim is to get down to fundamentals. But whereas in that poem and in *A Drunk Man* he celebrated multiplicity, in 'On a Raised Beach' he seeks the single rock – 'Alpha and Omega, the Omnific Word' – from which everything stems. He finds it in the stone in his hand and it has a frighteningly unhuman aspect:

> I am enamoured of the desert at last,
> The abode of supreme serenity is necessarily a desert.
> My disposition is towards spiritual issues
> Made inhumanly clear; I will have nothing interposed
> Between my sensitiveness and the barren but beautiful reality;
> The deadly clarity of this 'seeing of a hungry man'

(p.431)

(d)   Without doubt, 'On a Raised Beach' presents us with a

rigorous and unyielding view of the nature of truth, and it proposes
a disturbing conception of artistic creation –

> . . . freedom, precision and detachment
> A detachment that shocks our instincts and ridicules our desires

(p.426)

In these and in other ways it contains an illiberal and unforgiving
vision. G.S. Fraser has likened it to Carlyle's – the product, as it
were, of 'a very late type of Scottish Calvinist, seeking a God as
hard and testing and cold as rock'.[28] I am sure that you will have
found something of this tone in it, although, of course, it is not a
Christian God that MacDiarmid is seeking. The 'stupendous unity'
of his 'inoppugnable reality' has been brought down to the 'more
than Roman peace' of stone and death alike: 'Cold undistracted,
eternal and sublime'. The 'stoniness' of this world is conveyed
extremely impressively, but it has little to do with comfort,
forgiveness or resurrection.

Yet there is another side to the question, and that can be put as
follows. The poem is a thrilling experience of spiritual and
intellectual austerity. In the tradition of Christian ascetics (you may
care to compare this with Eliot's *Ash Wednesday*), the poet has
confronted the desert. MacDiarmid sees that the stones in the desert
are indifferent to man, and that in the cosmic scale of things, all
human life and art is not so much as a wisp of lichen on rock. (Which
takes us back to the 'fug o' fame and history's hazelraw' again.)
Furthermore, he is a materialist and so no promise of another life
can soften this view. Yet he accepts it and survives. He accepts
death; and he accepts that human potential is so far from being
fully realized that even our life is a kind of death for us anyway –
where we must always lose what is truly ours to take, because we
cannot rise to it:

> But let us not be afraid to die.
> No heavier and colder and quieter then,
> No more motionless, do stones lie
>   In death than in life to all men.
> It is not more difficult in death than here
> – Though slow as the stones the powers develop
> To rise from the grave – to get a life worth having;
> And in death – unlike life – we lose nothing that is truly ours.

(p.433)

In *Four Quartets*, Eliot's 'still point' offers hope of a spiritual life beyond physical existence; but MacDiarmid's stones insist on the irreducible materiality of the world. For the Marxist, there is nothing else. Yet the paradox is that the poem tries to make the realization and acceptance of that understanding an act of spiritual triumph in itself. These two long poems present fascinatingly different responses to the same basic anxieties. Would it be too much to call 'On a Raised Beach' a spiritual poem? Or does its rejection of any conception of the meaning of 'grace' and 'compassion' disqualify it entirely?

Part Three
1936–1978

Towards the Poetry of Fact and a Vision of World Language

We fumble along with partially bandaged eyes
Our reindeer-skin kamiks worn into holes
And no fresh sedge-grass to stump them with.
We come on ice-fields like mammoth ploughlands
And mountainous séracs which would puzzle an Alpine climber.
That is what adventuring in dictionaries means,
All the abysses and altitudes of the mind of man,
Every test and trial of the spirit,
Among the débris of all past literature
And raw material of all the literature to be.

('In Memoriam James Joyce', *Complete Poems*, p.823)

The Later Years

In the late thirties MacDiarmid worked on longer and longer poems, such as 'The Kind of Poetry I Want' and the three 'Direadh' pieces, parts of which first appeared in his autobiography *Lucky Poet* (he meant bad luck as well as good), published in 1943. It is an extraordinary collection of personal details, newspaper clippings, book reviews, letters, essays, poems, literary asides and jokes, with opinions and quotations about almost everything. Nothing more clearly, or infuriatingly, shows MacDiarmid's capacity as a polymath magpie, increasingly concerned at every turn, with 'man's incredible variation'.

This didactic, discursive and all-embracing outlook came to dominate MacDiarmid's creative energies as he attempted a complicated verse-epic synthesis of art, politics, linguistics and every kind of science. He planned a *magnum opus* to be called (variously) *Mature Art* or *Cornish Heroic Song for Valda Trevlyn*, although as a series of linked volumes of verse it was bound to be too long and too obscure to find easy publication, even without the problems of wartime printing. Nevertheless, committed to 'gigantism' in the arts and undaunted by its practical difficulties, MacDiarmid was to collate, rework and enlarge the various parts of his project throughout the rest of this, the third and last major stage of his imaginative life. Thus the section called *In Memoriam James Joyce* (which was itself billed as an extract from *A Vision of World Language*) was begun in 1939 but did not see publication until 1955; while *The Kind of Poetry I Want*, from the same period and the same overall scheme, did not achieve separate publication (even then incomplete) until 1961. In fact, this vast body of work was never drawn together during the poet's lifetime; critics are divided as to its value, and it presents the contemporary reader, as we shall see, with some fairly daunting aesthetic and theoretical challenges.

Called up to help the war effort in 1941, MacDiarmid left Whalsay early next year to live in Glasgow as a fitter making munitions at Mechans engineering works. In 1943 his legs were injured by a falling stack of copper cuttings and he had to transfer to the Merchant Navy. The poet spent the rest of the war as an engineer on board the *Gurli*, a service vessel for the British and American ships anchored in the Clyde estuary. His son Michael, who was thirteen when peace came, remembers those grey and cramped years in lodgings in Glasgow, and how his father sat late into every night labouring on the long 'world language' poems.

Hugh MacDiarmid working on the Clyde during World War II.
(Photo: Charles Nicol).

When the war ended, employment was difficult – MacDiarmid was fifty-three years old – but he managed to find work as a journalist again and threw himself into literary and political affairs. He stood (unsuccessfully) as an independent Nationalist candidate for Kelvingrove during the 1945 General Election, and revived *The Voice of Scotland*, a quarterly he had founded in 1938. Now there was a new generation of Scottish writers whose work, especially in poetry, made up what has been called the 'second wave' of the Scottish Renaissance. Sorley Maclean's collection *Dain do Eimhir*, ('Poems to Eimhir', 1943), had established him as the country's leading Gaelic poet, while William Soutar (who died tragically early), Sydney Goodsir Smith, Robert Garioch and Alexander Scott, had all produced fine poetry in Scots, matched by the English work of George Bruce, Norman MacCaig, Maurice Lindsay and, of course, Edwin Muir, although he would not have seen himself as part of that Northern movement.

The poetic harvest of this period was further enhanced in the fifties and sixties with the appearance of writers such as Tom Scott (in Scots), George Mackay Brown, Iain Crichton Smith (in Gaelic as well as English), George Campbell Hay (in Gaelic, Scots and English alike), Ian Hamilton Finlay, Edwin Morgan, and, in Gaelic alone, Derick Thomson. With the novels of Compton Mackenzie, Eric Linklater, Lewis Grassic Gibbon, Fionn MacColla, and Neil Gunn, and the plays of James Bridie, Robert McLellan and Alexander Reid, the literary 'renaissance' had been well and truly consolidated over a span of thirty years. Almost every one of these writers would have acknowledged that MacDiarmid's example had been central to a revival of creative confidence in the world of Scottish letters, and he continued to be a lively and pugnacious presence in their midst. Yet his own later poems did not gain a wide audience and many readers and critics felt that he had already done his best work.

Poems of the East-West Synthesis appeared in 1946, and *A Kist of Whistles* in the following year. Both collections expressed MacDiarmid's increasingly idiosyncratic hopes for international Socialism and a synthesis of all human knowledge and experience. He associated these goals with the revival or rediscovery of ancient Celtic values from Cornwall, Gaelic Scotland, Wales, Ireland, Brittany and, ultimately, the Caucasus and Asia Minor. Here he saw the 'golden wine' of an oral and heroic creative tradition whose mores were utterly at odds with the forces of capitalism and imperialism, which he believed had come to dominate the West. In this, MacDiarmid belongs very much in the company of Yeats,

Eliot and Pound, all of whom had felt compelled to find or create alternative systems of value, belief and mythic force for their art, in response, no doubt, to the prevailing disaffection of modern times. Aspects of this task were indeed well achieved by MacDiarmid, even if the lyrical conventions of what is usually regarded as 'poetry' were dispensed with along the way. On the other hand, the strident tone and the endless rant of a free verse polemical epic such as *The Battle Continues* (1957), testify to an egocentric and intolerant aspect of his voice, speaking from what seems to be an imaginative and political wilderness.

Certainly MacDiarmid's circumstances were spartan enough. A Civil List pension in 1950 helped him to make ends meet, and the following year a party of students from Edinburgh University modernized a tiny farmworker's cottage near Biggar, which was to be the poet's home for the rest of his life. As an increasingly well-known left-wing figure, he visited Russia in 1950, China in 1956, and several other European Socialist countries in 1959, in an international celebration of the bicentenary of Robert Burns's birth. He took part in political activities as an independent SNP candidate in 1950, and as a communist he stood against the Prime Minister, Sir Alec Douglas Hume, in 1964. Typically, he had rejoined the Communist Party after the invasion of Hungary in 1956, arguing that the basic tenets of Marxist-Leninism needed support, then more than ever. Such a gesture was more than controversial at a time when most party members in Britain and Europe were trying to dissociate themselves from the policies of Moscow.

The last twenty years of MacDiarmid's life brought him a growing number of honours. He was granted a doctorate from Edinburgh University in 1957 and membership of the Royal Scottish Academy in 1974, while visits to Canada, Italy and Ireland confirmed his standing among scholars abroad. He had come to be something of 'the grand old man', or more accurately perhaps, a distinguished fire-ship in the crowded harbour of Scottish letters. It must be admitted, however, that his work was granted less status and almost no serious analysis whatsoever from critics and literary historians in England, and this situation has still not changed very much. For many English readers, his use of Scots, his nationalism and his communism, have all, at different times, seemed like good reasons for mentioning his 'importance' before passing on to other things. Scholars in Scotland, America and even Europe have been quicker to give MacDiarmid his due, and many new studies have appeared in recent years. It seems inevitable that he will be granted a place – whatever his ranking – among the giants of the early modern period.

It was 1962, and the poet's seventieth year, before Macmillan of America produced the *Collected Poems* (there was a parallel British printing from Oliver and Boyd), and although it was nothing like a complete collection, it was the first time that most of MacDiarmid's major poems had been in print for many years. Two seminal critical studies appeared in 1964, and both books – by Kenneth Buthlay and Duncan Glen – did much to consolidate the poet's standing in academic and popular circles. A number of supplementary collections appeared in later years, but *A Lap of Honour* (1967), *A Clyack-Sheaf* (1969) and *More Collected Poems*, (1970), although useful at the time, are unsatisfactory from a bibliographical point of view. At least *In Memoriam James Joyce* from 1955, and *The Kind of Poetry I Want* in 1961, bore some consistent connection with earlier plans for the epic *Mature Art*. The poet had not added to this canon for many years, but the problems of selecting and editing work from it still remain formidable. The two volume *Complete Poems 1920–1976* made an advance in this direction and remains the definitive edition, but, sadly, the poet never saw its publication, for he died of cancer in September 1978. He was eighty-six. Frail for several years and seriously ill at the end, MacDiarmid never broke contact with the wide circle of his interests and correspondents, nor lost his iconoclastic delight in the clash of opinions and the excitement of ideas: 'I like to savour them one after the other. . . but do not commit myself to any of them', he wrote in one of his last letters, adding, with a characteristically dry spark, 'A stance of moral anarchy, of course.'[29]

The Gaelic Muse and Epic Art

From his vantage point in Whalsay, and far from the mainstream of popular reputation, MacDiarmid numbered writers such as Charles Doughty and John Davidson among his heroes and literary predecessors. It seemed to him that in their style and epic scope these nearly forgotten men had truly met Hardy's challenge to find a 'written expression of revolt against accepted things', or Rilke's demand that a poet should 'know everything'. He admired the idiosyncratically rugged verse of Doughty's multi-volume opus *The Dawn in Britain* (1906); while the prose of *Travels in Arabia Deserta* (1988), had shown a commitment to inhospitably remote and desert places that perfectly symbolized MacDiarmid's understanding of a true artist's proper realm.[30] He shared Doughty's feeling for the harsh intensity of 'the seeing of a hungry man' (the phrase comes from *Arabia Deserta*), and this note is evident

Portrait of Hugh MacDiarmid, 1970. (Photo: Duncan Glen).

throughout 'On a Raised Beach'. Indeed, the title poem of *Stony Limits* had been dedicated to the English traveller, for MacDiarmid looked to his example (as to the equally arcane art of Joyce and Pound), for the polyglot and self-consciously 'scientific' diction of poems such as 'In the Caledonian Forest' and 'Etika Preobrazhennavo Erosa'.

John Davidson was equally uncompromising in the pursuit of his art. He was a Scot in London who committed suicide in 1909 when his mature poems failed to find the success granted to his early work. Davidson believed that poetry should 'certify the semi-certitudes of science', and his later free verse attempted to do this by linking scientific topics and vocabulary to his own vision of matter's long evolution towards higher and higher consciousness. (See, for example, his poem *The Testament of John Davidson*, 1908.) Thus, for Davidson, the stones on MacDiarmid's beach, the stars above them, the chemical composition of seaweed and man's cerebral processes would all be manifestations of the same fundamental drive. This unified vision of the physical world was very much in line with MacDiarmid's own feelings. It goes back to the psychological solipsism of the stories in *Annals of the Five Senses*; it reflects the Romantic egocentricity of *A Drunk Man*; and it makes a perfect reconciliation between these works and the poet's later commitment to scientific materialism.[31] MacDiarmid remembered his debt to Davidson in an essay from 1961[32]; and an elegy from 1932, 'Of John Davidson', recalls 'one death in my boyhood / That next to my father's, and darker, endures'.

In pursuit of this new understanding of art in epic, rather than lyrical terms, MacDiarmid began to cite the example of Gaelic poetry, and in particular the eighteenth-century descriptive verses of Alasdair MacMhaighstir Alasdair and Duncan Bàn Macintyre. With the help of his young friend Sorley Maclean, MacDiarmid translated their two most famous works – namely, MacMhaighstir Alasdair's 'The Birlinnof Clanranald' ('Clanranald's Galley'), and Duncan Bàn's 'The Praise of Ben Dorain'. Both poems rise to very subtle and complex rhythms, assonances and verse structures, which MacDiarmid worked hard to convey; yet his own poetry of this period is almost always in English free verse. Nevertheless, he proposed a 'Gaelic' voice for himself in poems such as 'Lament for the Great Music' (1934), or the 'Direadh' pieces and 'The Gaelic Muse', from 1939. Let us consider, for a moment, what he was seeking. What qualities can you identify, for example, in the following passage from 'Direadh III'?

Here near the summit of Sgurr Alasdair*
The air is very still and warm,
The Outer Isles look as though
They were cut out of black paper
And stuck on a brilliant silver background,
(Even as I have seen the snow-capped ridges of Hayes Peninsula
Stand out stark and clear in the pellucid Arctic atmosphere
Or, after a wild and foggy night, in the dawn
Seen the jagged line of the Tierra del Fuego cliffs
Looking for all the world as if they were cut out of tin,
Extending gaunt and desolate),
The western sea and sky undivided by horizon,
So dazzling is the sun
And its glass image in the sea.
The Cuillin peaks seem miniature
And nearer than is natural
And they move like liquid ripples
In the molten breath
Of the corries which divide them.
I light my pipe and the match burns steadily
Without the shielding of my hands,
The flame hardly visible in the intensity of light
Which drenches the mountain top.

(*Complete Poems*, pp.1186–7)

* The highest peak of the dramatically severe Cuillin range in Skye.

DISCUSSION

I find these lines very effective, despite the fact that they do seem to operate at a low imaginative pressure. The similes of tin and black and silver paper are stated with a prose-like simplicity and modesty, as only one among several observations whose unforced openness is echoed by the simple grammar – 'the Outer Isles look. . .'; 'the Cuillin peaks seem . . . And they move like. . .'; and then, 'I light my pipe and the match burns steadily. . .'. This effect is often found in passages of *In Memoriam James Joyce*, (see, for example, pp.756–9, or pp.821–3 in the *Complete Poems*, sometimes titled as 'In the Fall' and 'The Task'). Such 'pellucid' clarity is very strikingly different from the voice in MacDiarmid's early Scots lyrics, in which an expressionist energy invaded every atom of the landscape, as we saw, for example, in 'Farmer's Death' and 'On an Ill-Faur'd Star'. Finally, the poet's allusions to the far North and South America have a certain formal quality, not unlike a classical allusion or an epic simile, for in context, we soon understand that this is a matter of impersonal reference rather than any more literal claim to be a daring explorer.

In fact, what MacDiarmid has taken from his interest in Gaelic art is a sense of epic detachment. This is conveyed through a special kind of passionate objectivity, as if poetic description were an intense and relatively selfless act which does not seek to invest the landscape with Romantic shades of the writer's own psyche. Both MacMhaighstir Alasdair and Duncan Bàn are famous for the specific details that they incorporate into their verse – Alasdair's knowledge of boats and weather, for example, and Duncan Bàn's incomparable appreciation of everything to do with deer on the hills, how they feed, and how one hunts them. The cool passion of such expertise moved MacDiarmid, and he wanted to achieve it in his own poetry. It was all the more satisfying that such a point of view could be defined as 'Celtic', utterly unlike any English mode, and of course he had been in favour of such developments since his *Chapbook* days.[33]

'Let me play to you tunes without measure or end', the poet wrote in 'Bagpipe Music' (p.665), 'As a flight of storks rises from a marsh, circles, / And alights on the spot from which it rose'. These lines indicate what MacDiarmid's long poems owe to the spirit of pibroch, although their free verse structure does not follow the intricate formal patterns of the music itself. What caught the poet's imagination was the concept of an art that ended where it began (with its tail in its mouth), after having gone through ever more elaborate variations on a single theme. Thus, for example, the 'theme' of 'The Kind of Poetry I Want' is quite simply conveyed by its title, while the verses are the 'variations', namely an inexhaustible list of different examples drawn from the most diverse sources.

Consider the passage below in the light of this. What do these examples have in common, and can they be related to MacDiarmid's earlier work?

> A poetry full of erudition, expertise, and ecstasy
> – The acrobatics and the faceted fly-like vision,
> The transparency choke-full of hair-pin bends,
> 'Jacinth work of subtlest jewellery', poetry *à quatre épingles* – *
> (Till above every line we might imagine
> A tensely flexible and complex curve
> Representing the modulation,
> Emphasis, and changing tone and tempo
> Of the voice in reading;
> The curve varying from line to line
> And the lines playing subtly against one another
> – A fineness and profundity of organisation
> Which is the condition of a variety great enough

To express all the world's,
As subtle and complete and tight
As the integration of the thousands of brush strokes
In a Cézanne canvas),
Alive as a bout of all-in wrestling,
With countless illustrations like my photograph of a Mourning Dove
Taken at a speed of 1/75,000 of a second,
A poetry that speaks 'of trees,
From the Cedar tree that is in Lebanon
Even unto the hyssop that springeth out of the wall',
And speaks also 'of beasts and of fowl,
And of creeping things, and of fishes'+

(p.1019)

* 'dressed to the nines'
+Wise King Solomon speaks of these things in Kings I:4:33.

The poem proceeds in this fashion at great length, for its method is to present us with an extended catalogue of analogies. They may seem familiar, in spirit at least, for what they all have in common is 'the movement that a'thing shares'. In other words, I would argue, they are further manifestations of the 'water of life', or the drunk man's old quarry, the sea serpent. But this time the poet truly has broken free 'o' my eternal me', and he has come at last to ennumerate the variety of the world simply for its own sake. He does not discount inner experience of course, but his new found 'disinterestedness' has gained peace and a selflessly expanded scope among the thousands of books he had never ceased to devour, from his earliest days in a house below the Langholm Public Library.

The Poetry of Fact

MacDiarmid began to call such verse a 'poetry of fact', by which he meant not just a poetry with facts in it, but the poetry inherent *in* 'facts'. To support his case, he claimed that it was the task of the true communist to 'work over' in his own consciousness 'the whole inheritance of human knowledge', agreeing with Plekhanov that 'the quality of a work of art is, in the final analysis, determined by the "specific gravity", as it were, of its content'. The poet also liked to quote Walt Whitman's assertion that writers should 'conform with and build on the concrete realities and theories of the universe furnished by science, and henceforth the only irrefragable basis for anything, verse included'. These matters were all raised early in *Lucky Poet*, which was itself something of a 'cyclotron' of 'immense erudition' for 'bombarding' people with knowledge and, as he put it in typically buccaneering fashion, for shocking 'the appalling mindlessness of almost everybody'. With the same iconoclastic end in view, he quoted Ouspensky to claim that 'imagination runs away with our thoughts and leads a thoroughly destructive life within us. . . We can only stop the wasteful chase of our imagination by being attentive. The moment we are attentive the activities of our imagination cease, and *thought* can come into action'[34] (my emphasis).

Thus it was that MacDiarmid, who had achieved such splendid linguistic and imaginative leaps in *A Drunk Man* and the early lyrics, came to favour instead a long and diligent 'attentiveness'. It is as if the writer had relinquished his image-*making* power (which is how Coleridge and the Romantics defined poetry in the first place), in favour of a humbler role. The Romantic explorer has given way to a learned cataloguer in the library of the world, who shows us round and recites lists of all that there is in it, looking to the communal epic tradition of Homer and that list of boats on the beach at Troy, rather than to the visionary dreams of 'Kubla Khan'. In this respect, MacDiarmid's new understanding of his muse took him forward to his interest in reconciling science and poetry, and back in time to the impersonal function of the bard as a man who remembered and recited things, thus reaffirming them in the mind of the community:

> The rarity and value of scientific knowledge
> Is little understood – even as people
> Who are not botanists find it hard to believe
> Special knowledge of the subject can add
> Enormously to the aesthetic appreciation of flowers!
> Partly because in order to identify a plant
> You must study it very much more closely
> Than you would otherwise have done, and in the process
> Exquisite colours, proportions, and minute changes spring to light
> Too small to be ordinarily noted.

(from 'Poetry and Science', *Complete Poems*, p.630)

The objectivity of these recited 'facts' is further guaranteed – ironically enough – when we realize that many passages in these later poems have been taken without acknowledgement from other sources – usually in prose. Thus, for example, seven lines in the passage from 'The Kind of Poetry I Want' quoted on page 90 above, come straight from *Revaluations*, in which F.R. Leavis gives an account of Pope's poetry as compared to Dryden's. (They run from 'Till above every line. . .' to '. . .subtly against one another'.) This has led to various critical problems in the assessment of the poems of fact, not least to some debate as to whether they are poems at all![35]

The matter of literary 'borrowing' without acknowledgement is a tender issue, and while we can enjoy Eliot's *bon mot* to the effect that minor poets borrow and great ones *steal*, it does not help to resolve the moral, and even legal complications that arise.[36] Then there are the critical questions of what happens when a piece of creative, discursive or technical prose is re-cast as 'poetry'. Do we read it differently? Do the lines in an 'aesthetic' context have a more aesthetically pleasing effect? Such questions arose with particular force when MacDiarmid's poem 'Perfect' was found to be largely drawn from a short story by Welsh writer Glyn Jones. In fact, the lines in question had first been used as an epigraph to a chapter in MacDiarmid's *The Islands of Scotland*, from whence it found its way into the canon of his verse. When all this came to light, there was a fascinating debate in the *Times Literary Supplement*, from January to May, 1965. W.B. Yeats touched on similar issues in the introduction to his edition of the *Oxford Book of Modern Verse 1892–1935*, when he set a passage of Walter Pater's prose as a poem called 'Mona Lisa'.

There is no doubt that we do experience 'poetry' in a different way from 'prose', and you may care to take the matter further with reference to contemporary critical approaches such as 'reception theory'.[37] For the moment, let us propose that the question of 'authorship' is circumvented to a certain extent in MacDiarmid's later verses, because they have left behind the concept of the poem as an originally inspired, finely wrought, and *concluded* work. Indeed, the poet has relinquished his role as controller of metaphors and god-like author, in favour of a more open-ended, and less structured relationship between himself, the text and the reader. Such a position is in line with contemporary developments in critical theory and, to some extent, with achievements in American poetry, from Ezra Pound's *Cantos* to the work of William Carlos Williams, Charles Olsen, and, more recently, John Ashbery. In this spirit, MacDiarmid's later poetry seems to ignore the artistic arrangement of words, in order to make them more 'transparent' and to point beyond themselves to the 'things' of the world. Then again, other poems of his seem to focus on language for what it represents *as language itself*. Thus, for MacDiarmid at least, both words *and* things are an interchangable 'vocabulary', as it were, from a more complex, elusive, fundamental and unified perception of universal process.

Hence the 'world language' that MacDiarmid celebrates in *In*

Memoriam James Joyce, seems to me to be both the world *of* language, and the world itself as if *it* were a kind of language, too. The extensive lists of words, books, people, things, events and descriptions in the poem, are the product of a mind that has come to see them all, equally and simply, as *signs*: and the 'creative' poetic task has been reinterpreted as a matter of bearing witness to these signs by enunciating them. Consider, for example, two different poems, which work to a similar end: namely the passage 'Let the only consistency. . .' from *In Memoriam James Joyce*, which was first printed as 'In the Fall' (p.756), and the poem 'Diamond Body' (pp.1084–8). You might like to read them before going further.

DISCUSSION

Both pieces offer extended descriptions of natural detail. What do you make of this, and are there differences in treatment between them? This is from 'In the Fall':

> So I think of you, Joyce, and of Yeats and others who are dead
> As I walk this Autumn and observe
> The birch tremulously pendulous in jewels of cairngorm,
> the sauch, the osier, and the crack-willow
> Of the beaten gold of Australia;
> The sycamore in rich straw-gold;
> The elm bowered in saffron;
> The oak in flecks of salmon gold;
> The beeches huge torches of living orange.
>
> Billow upon billow of autumnal foliage
> From the sheer high bank glass themselves
> Upon the ebon and silver curent that floods freely
> Past the shingle shelves.
> I linger where a crack willow slants across the stream,
> Its olive leaves slashed with fine gold.
> Beyond the willow a young beech
> Blazes almost blood-red,
> Vying in intensity with the glowing cloud of crimson
> That hangs about the purple bole of a gean
> Higher up the brae face.

(pp.757–8)

First of all, one cannot help being struck by the diction of this passage, with its emphasis on 'jewels', 'cairngorm', 'beaten gold', 'ebon' and 'silver' – all of which bring a lapidary quality to the scene, emphasizing a certain richness, formality and artifice. Then again, '*straw*-gold', 'saffron', 'salmon', 'olive', and 'glowing cloud' compound that sense of richness with wholesome terms drawn from the living world. Then the effect is heightened and formalized again by 'huge torches' and colours of 'living orange', 'blood-red', 'crimson' and 'purple'. Against such splendour, it is little wonder that we lose the darker implications of death and Autumn, and the poem comes to seem like a triumphal pageant instead.

If you were bothered by the stiffly 'poetic' vocabulary of 'bowered', 'billow upon billow', and that extraordinary locution – 'tremulously pendulous', I would defend it by pointing to the overall effect of the passage, which is, indeed, formal and stately, rather like the 'enamelled' rhetoric of Dunbar's nature descriptions from the late fifteenth century. Against this immensely static effect, one has to set a curiously contradictory *intensity* in the scene, evidenced by the active implications in such words as 'tremulous', 'billow', 'floods freely', 'slants', 'slashed', 'blazes', 'vying' and, finally, 'glowing'. On the other hand, it is here that the poet 'lingers' and 'observes', and the passage is itself, after all, a leisurely catalogue of 'the birch', 'the sauch, the osier, the crack-willow', 'the sycamore', 'the elm', 'the beeches' and 'the oak', which are offered to us as a syntactically simple and affectionate list. The detached tone is reminiscent of how lists appear in the Bible or in epic verse, and it returns us again to the formal nature of the poet's approach. The overall effect is to bring personal and stylistic 'disinterestedness' alongside a ferocious eye for 'blazing' detail.

The elevated simplicity of MacDiarmid's approach and the formality of his English diction, are reminiscent of Wordsworth's voice in parts of *The Prelude*, and indeed the landscape of 'In the Fall' is a Romantic image in familiar style – for the splendour and inexhaustible richness of the scene is used to symbolize the survival of creative life beyond the death of any individual artist. By comparison, the more neutrally 'scientific' vocabulary of 'Diamond Body' takes a quite different route to the same end; and the difference is a crucial one, for it begins to leave the lyric voice – however stately and dispassionate – rather far behind. The poem is set 'in a cave of the sea':

> What after all do we know of this terrible 'matter'
> Save as a name for the unknown and hypothetical cause
> Of states of our own consciousness? There are not two worlds,
> A world of nature, and a world of human consciousness,
> Standing over against one another, but one world of nature
> Whereof human consciousness is an evolution,
> I reminded myself again as I caught that sudden breathless glimpse,

Under my microscope, of unexpected beauty and dynamic living
In the world of life on a silver of kelp. . .
And, in a rock pool, 'crumb of bread' sponge,
Hydroids, red, green, purple, or richly patterned
Like the dahlia anemone, yellow sea-lemon, and now and again
A rapidly moving snail shell which shows me
It is inhabited by a hermit crab
Much more active than its original occupant.
Countless millions of creatures each essential
To that other, and precisely fashioned
In every detail to meet his requirements.
Millions upon millions of them
Hardly discernible here
In the brilliant light in which sea and sky
Can hardly be distinguished from each other
– And I know there are billions more
Too small for a man to see
Even though human life were long enough
To see them all, a process that can hardly
Be even begun.

(pp.1084–5, 1086)

The rich colours have survived – 'red, green, purple' – but the poet's diction is much more prosaic, less willing to draw attention to its creative powers and more willing to offer the neutral precision (you may think it scholarly or merely pedantic), of remarks such as 'much more active than its original occupant'. Some readers would maintain that this more 'prosaic' verse – perhaps with passages taken directly from text books – simply reflects the failure of MacDiarmid's creative powers, and it cannot be denied that the *Mature Art* volumes do contain long and tedious stretches. Yet this is not the whole point, and in defence of MacDiarmid's vision, a passage from Wordsworth's preface to the 1805 edition of *Lyrical Ballads* suggests itself. Wordsworth is claiming that 'the poet binds together by passion and *knowledge*, [my emphasis] the vast empire of human society':

> If the labours of men of science should ever create any material revolution. . . in the impressions which we habitually receive, the poet will sleep then no more than at present. . . The remotest discoveries of the chemist, the botanist, or mineralogist will be as proper objects of the poet's art as any upon which it can be employed, if the time should ever come when these things shall be familiar to us . . . as enjoying and suffering beings.

MacDiarmid would say that such a time *had* come. Even so, he has not entirely relinquished the poet's duty to 'aid the trans figuration' of things, as Wordsworth put it, and the poem's title, 'Diamond

Body' reminds us that it comes to a climax of spiritual insight. Indeed, we have met the 'brilliant light' of the passage above in MacDiarmid's poems before. It was present on the raised beach; and on the summit of Sgurr Alasdair; and in many of the lyrics, going back as far as 'A Moment in Eternity', a very early visionary poem in English, which experienced 'white light like a silence', in which 'each gesture' and 'each shining shadow of difference' was set free and resolved in overwhelming mystical unity.

A Vision of World Language

Yeats held that poetry came from the 'argument' that we have with ourselves, and this is particularly true, although in a different sense, perhaps, in the case of MacDiarmid's later world language poems. In them, the verse itself describes its own theory, and language itself becomes only another metaphor for the universal in the local. So it is that language's most technical and arcane usages, like the specialized crafts and skills from which they stem, are used to symbolize the endless complexity in unity which he had so long pursued:

> Hardy with words like lewth, leazes, dumble-dores,
> Spuds, cit, wanzing, and his trained architect's use
> Of adze, cusp, ogee, and the like: and, again,
> Fantocine, junctive law, foresightlessness,
> Meredith's specialised philosophical vocabulary,
> 'Yaffles on a chuckle skim,'
> 'Heaven a space for winging tons,'
> Uttering a secret language as if in the belief
> That it was a universal speech, yet even if
> A secret language it contains a body
> Of thought and intuitions worth unravelling.
> . . .
> Doughty, by far the greatest of them all . . .
> Writing of ogival arches, traps, and basalt,
> But equally ready when it comes to the pasterns of a horse,
> The tilts of a camel-litter,
> The nombril of a shield,
> The burdon of a pilgrim:
> Knowing that squirrel's *drey* is better than squirrel's *nest*,
> Making language at once more rich and more precise,
> And passionate for naming particular things
> And particular parts of things,
> So he writes of a *shive* of wood, *shivers* of silvex,
> Of a *gripe*, a *thrave*, and a *strike* of corn . . .
>
> (from *In Memoriam James Joyce*, pp.739–40)

In other passages from the same long poem MacDiarmid cites

Jesperson, Saussure and the Russian Formalists in recognizing an essentially structuralist position on the absolute primacy of language, especially, of course, in literature:

> For in the aesthetic experience
> Instead of language meaning the material of experience
> – Things, ideas, emotions, feelings –
> This material means language.

(p.752)

So it is not just the world which is a model for language to imitate, but language itself, with all its complexities and strange byways, is the first and only pattern by which we know the world. In this, his latest of many manifestations, the curly snake has indeed turned entirely into *words*, which alone, (by definition, after all) have a 'variety great enough to express all the world's'. So the 'world language' poems offer us both the world-as-language and language-as-the-world.

Conclusion

At the end of the section called 'In the Fall', MacDiarmid had this to say:

> They are not endless these variations of form
> Though it is perhaps impossible to see them all.
> It is certainly impossible to conceive one that doesn't exist.
> But I keep trying in our forest to do both of these,
> And though it is a long time now since I saw a new one
> I am by no means weary yet . . .

(p.758)

The pursuit should be familiar now, for those variations of form have been with us from the very start. When their unity was desired (in poetry, philosophy, politics, or social life) MacDiarmid sought them as the 'rose', the 'seamless garment' and the 'impossible song'; and when their elusive multiplicity was to the fore, they appeared as the 'sea serpent' in a hundred guises.[38]

Now lyric poetry and the poetic metaphor offer an imaginative transformation of material, so that the essence of the situation is grasped in a single, selective, intuitive leap; and MacDiarmid made these leaps magnificently vividly in *A Drunk Man* and the early mature work. But the later poems would not settle for such selectivity and, in their search for a selfless and timeless epic mode, they adopted the catalogue, rather than the metaphor as their controlling guide. With this model there can be no end to the process, just as there is no end to the process of life itself, and MacDiarmid pursued the logic of his choice into longer and longer poems, and sometimes, too, into greater and greater obscurity, like some Charles Doughty crossing vastly inhospitable literary deserts.

Yet the poet's search for the innumerable threads of his seamless garment has been logical, perhaps inevitable, and his uncompromising journey can tell us much about language, poetry, and the philosophical problems of idealism in life and literature. In fact, MacDiarmid's final vision of the world breaks down the conventional borders between 'art' and 'not art', and such reductiveness may seem to disturb or overthrow more conventional notions of what culture is. Yet, at least to the poet's way of looking at it, the vision is creative and life-enhancing, for it brings together the brush strokes of a Cézanne painting and the humble stones on a beach, and offers them both to us, if we will only lose our preconceptions, as powerful icons for the interrelationship between the human spirit and the material world.

This journey may have taken him to the end of 'art' as it is understood in those post-Renaissance and post-Romantic terms, which place such a high value (not least a financial one) on the striking productions of the individual soul. But his journey never led him to despair of man, or man's knowledge, or to doubt his capacity to change himself and his society; nor did it lead, at least in the end, to alienation, pessimism and cultural anguish in his poetry. Yet these ailments have been rife in modern art, and nowhere more strikingly than among MacDiarmid's poetic contemporaries, Yeats, Eliot and Pound, who, like him, were big enough to face and to feel the issues of our time.

If I have to summarize my respect for MacDiarmid's iconoclastic and creative optimism, in a period when such qualities were rare indeed, I think of Blake whose sense of cosmic scale allowed him, too, to find eternity in an hour and a world in a grain of sand, and who was equally committed to a reconciliation and a celebration of both the base and the beautiful, of the material world and the world of the spirit. These lines from 'The Marriage of Heaven and Hell' (c.1793) could have been specifically written to convey the tenor of MacDiarmid's work through a long and varied career:

1   Man has no Body distinct from his Soul; for that call'd Body is a portion of Soul discern'd by the five Senses, the chief inlets of Soul in this age.

2   Energy is the only life, and is from the Body; and Reason is the bound or outward circumference of Energy.

3   Energy is Eternal delight.

Notes and References

Introduction

1   Leon Shestov, *In Job's Balances*, trans. C. Coventry and C.A.
    Macartney, London, 1932, pp.225–6. See *Lucky Poet*, (1943),
    London, Jonathan Cape, 1972, p.67.
2   This tradition is well outlined, for example, by Kurt Wittig in *The
    Scottish Tradition in Literature*, Edinburgh, Oliver and Boyd, 1958.

Part One

3   'The Waterside' (1927), in Kenneth Buthlay (Ed.), *The Uncanny Scot.
    A Selection of Prose by Hugh MacDiarmid*, London, Macgibbon &
    Kee, 1968, pp.42–3. See also 'My Native Place' (1931), in Duncan
    Glen (Ed.), *Selected Essays of Hugh MacDiarmid*, London, Jonathan
    Cape, 1969, p.53.
4   Hugh MacDiarmid, *Lucky Poet*, p.10.
5   'Hugh MacDiarmid's Early Poetry', in Duncan Glen (Ed.), *Hugh
    MacDiarmid: A Critical Survey*, Edinburgh, Scottish Academic Press,
    1972, p.65. (Henceforth: *A Critical Survey*.)
6   Kenneth Buthlay, *Hugh MacDiarmid*, Edinburgh, Scottish Academic
    Press, 1982, pp.28–9.
7   Peter Jones (Ed.) *Imagist Poetry*, London, Penguin, 1972, p.48.
8   See K. Duval and S.G. Smith (Eds), *Hugh MacDiarmid: A Festschrift*,
    Edinburgh, K.D. Duval, 1962, p.59.
9   T.S. Eliot, *Collected Poems 1909–1962*, London, Faber, 1963,
    pp.27–8.
10 See Edwin Morgan, 'Poetry and Knowledge in MacDiarmid's Later
    Work' in *A Critical Survey*, p.192.
11 Iain Crichton Smith, 'The Golden Lyric', in *A Critical Survey*, pp.139–
    140.
12 Frank Kermode and John Hollander (Eds), *Modern British Literature:
    The Oxford Anthology of English Literature*, London, Oxford
    University Press, 1973, p.563.
13 A more detailed exposition can be found in my essay 'The Symbolism

of *A Drunk Man Looks at the Thistle'*, in *A Critical Survey*, p.94.

14 See Leon Shestov, *All Things Are Possible*, S.S. Koteliansky (Trans.), London, 1920, p.110.

15 *Scottish Literature: Character and Influence*, London, Macmillan, 1919.

Part Two

16 Eric Linklater painted an amusingly satirical portrait of him as 'Hugh Skene' in his novel *Magnus Merriman* (1934). Early office-holders in the National Party had connections with the ILP, and in 1934 it merged with the Scottish Party to form the present day Scottish National Party.

17 Discussed at length in Roderick Watson, ' "Water Music" and the Stream of Consciousness', in *Scottish Literary Journal*, (MacDiarmid Memorial Number), Aberdeen, 5 (2), December 1978. p.6.

18 *Lucky Poet*, p.41.

19 'Hugh MacDiarmid: The Man' in *The Hugh MacDiarmid Anthology*, London, Routledge and Kegan Paul, 1972, p.xi.

20 Stephen Maxwell, 'The Nationalism of Hugh MacDiarmid'; Neal Ascherson, 'MacDiarmid and Politics', in P.H. Scott and A.C. Davis (Eds), *The Age of MacDiarmid*, Edinburgh, Mainstream Publishing, 1980.

21 In Robin Skelton (Ed.), *Poetry of the Thirties*, Penguin, 1964, pp.80–1.

22 Iain Crichton Smith, 'MacDiarmid and Ideas', *The Age of MacDiarmid*, pp.157–62.

23 David Craig, 'MacDiarmid the Marxist Poet', in *A Critical Survey*, p.155.

24 Kenneth Buthlay is much more critical of what he calls the poem's 'sentimental bourgeois ambience': 'Some Hints for Source-hunters', in *Scottish Literary Journal*, 5 (2), December 1978, pp. 58–9.

25 For further reading, the poem is usefully discussed by G.S. Fraser in his essay 'The Later Poetry' in *A Critical Survey*, and Catherine Kerrigan deals with it at the close of her book *Whaur Extremes Meet*, Edinburgh, James Thin, 1983. Further discussion can be found in Alan Bold, *MacDiarmid: The Terrible Crystal*, London, Routledge, 1983; in Iain Crichton Smith, 'MacDiarmid and Ideas', in *The Age of MacDiarmid*; and Ruth McQuillan, 'Hugh MacDiarmid's "On a Raised Beach" ', *Akros*, 12, (34–35). Finally, the eminent philosopher D.M. Mackinnon invokes it in *The Problem of Metaphysics*, London, Cambridge University Press, 1974, pp.164–8.

26 *The Uncanny Scot: a selection of prose by Hugh MacDiarmid*, London, MacGibbon and Kee, 1968, p.90.

27 Fraser and Daiches have offered glosses, and Ruth McQuillan has traced the poet's specific debt to *Chambers Twentieth Century Dictionary*, see 'MacDiarmid's Other Dictionary', *Lines Review*, Edinburgh, 66, September 1978.

28 In *A Critical Survey*, p.219.

Part Three

29   Alan Bold (Ed.), *The Letters of Hugh MacDiarmid*, London, Hamish
      Hamilton, 1984, p.889.
30   See 'Charles Doughty and the Need for Heroic Poetry' (1936), in
      Selected Essays of Hugh MacDiarmid, p.75.
31   MacDiarmid had found similar ideas about the world's evolution
      towards consciousness – towards God in this case – in the thoughts of
      the Russian philosopher Vladimir Solovyov.
32   'John Davidson: Influences and Influence', *Selected Essays*, p.197.
33   A further discussion of MacDiarmid's later involvement with the
      Gaelic ethos can be found in Douglas Sealy, 'Hugh MacDiarmid and
      Gaelic Literature', in *A Critical Survey*, p.168.
34   For all these views, see *Lucky Poet*, pp.xxxi–ii; pp.407–8; p.xxxiv.
35   For further reading on this issue, consider Edwin Morgan, 'Poetry and
      Knowledge in MacDiarmid's Later Work', in *A Critical Survey*, p.192,
      as well as 'MacDiarmid's later poetry against an international
      background', by the same author in *Scottish Literary Journal*, 5 (2),
      December 1978, p.20. Further stimulating points are made in the same
      journal by Kenneth Buthlay with 'Some Hints for Source-hunters',
      p.50; while Iain Crichton Smith takes a less sympathetic line, as
      already noted in his essays on 'The Golden Lyric' and 'MacDiarmid
      and Ideas'.
36   Richard Ellman's book, *Eminent Domain* (London, Oxford University
      Press, 1967), provides entertaining and informative insights on this
      topic.
37   See, for example, Wolfgang Iser, *The Act of Reading*, London,
      Routledge and Kegan Paul, 1978.
38   R.B. Watson, 'A Critical Study of the "Cencrastus Theme" in the
      Poetry of Hugh MacDiarmid', Diss. Cambridge, 1970.

Further Reading and a Select Bibliography

Works in Prose and Verse by Hugh MacDiarmid

MACDIARMID, HUGH, *(1978) Complete Poems 1920–1976*, M. Grieve and W.R. Aitken (Eds), 2 Vols. London, Martin Brian and O'Keeffe. (1985) Published in paperback by Penguin Books with the addition of corrections and an Appendix.
[A definitive collection of almost every poem Mac-Diarmid wrote.]

(1972) *The Hugh MacDiarmid Anthology*, M. Grieve and A. Scott (Eds), London, Routledge and Kegan Paul.

(1970) *Hugh MacDiarmid. Selected Poems*, D. Craig and J. Manson (Eds). Harmondsworth, Penguin.

(1978) *The Socialist Poems of Hugh MacDiarmid*, T.S. Law and T. Berwick (Eds), London, Routledge & Kegan Paul.
[Three useful selections of poems, all slightly lacking in examples from the early lyrics.]

(1968) *The Uncanny Scot. A Selection of Prose by Hugh MacDiarmid*, K. Buthlay (Ed.), London, Macgibbon and Kee.

(1969) *Selected Essays of Hugh MacDiarmid.* D. Glen (Ed.), London, Jonathan Cape.
[Two indispensable selections from MacDiarmid's creative, and more especially in the latter volume, his discursive prose.]

(1972) *Lucky Poet*, London, Jonathan Cape. (First published, 1943)

(1966) *The Company I've Kept*, London, Hutchinson.
[The latter volume is a continuation of the poet's massive and eclectic autobiography.]

(1976) *Contemporary Scottish Studies.* Edinburgh, the Scottish Educational Journal.

[A reissue with additional material of essays first collected in 1926 from the *Scottish Educational Journal*, and a good example of the poet's early critical activities and the heated correspondence they engendered.]

(1983)   *Annals of the Five Senses*, A. Bold (Ed.), Edinburgh, Polygon Books. [First published in 1923, but written several years earlier, these few poems and six 'psychological studies' in creative prose offer a key insight to MacDiarmid's sensibility.]

(1939)   *The Islands of Scotland*, London, B.T. Batsford. [Essays on the Hebrides, Orkney and Shetland, written while on Whalsay.]

(1984)   *The Letters of Hugh MacDiarmid*, A. Bold (Ed.), London, Hamish Hamilton.
[A large and invaluable collection of the poet's letters, arranged by correspondent and well indexed and annotated.]

Critical Studies

BUTHLAY, K. *(1964) Hugh MacDiarmid (C.M. Grieve)*. Edinburgh and London, Oliver and Boyd, Writers and Critics. (1982) Revised, enlarged edition. Edinburgh, Scottish Academic Press.

GLEN, D. (1964) *Hugh MacDiarmid and the Scottish Renaissance*, Edinburgh and London, W. and R. Chambers.

[These two books were key early studies of MacDiarmid's work and still have much to offer. The Glen volume includes discussion of the wider cultural scene.]

DUVAL, K. and S.G. SMITH (Eds) (1962) *Hugh MacDiarmid: A Festschrift*, Edinburgh, K.D. Duval.

GLEN, D. (Ed.) (1972) *Hugh MacDiarmid: A Critical Survey*, Edinburgh, Scottish Academic Press.

[Glen's most useful edition reprints five essays from the *Festschrift* along with new material and an updated Bibliography by W.R. Aitken.]

SCOTT, P.H. and DAVIS A.C. (Eds) (1980) *The Age of MacDiarmid*, Edinburgh, Mainstream Publishing.

[Memories, appreciations and wider reflections on the poet and his time.]

BOLD, A. (1983) *MacDiarmid: The Terrible Crystal*, London, Routledge.

BOUTELLE, A.E. (1981) *Thistle and Rose. A Study of Hugh MacDiarmid's Poetry*, Edinburgh, Macdonald.

KERRIGAN, C. (1983). *Whaur Extremes Meet. The poetry of Hugh MacDiarmid 1920–1934*, Edinburgh, James Thin.

GISH, N. (1984) *Hugh MacDiarmid. The Man and his Work*, London, Macmillan.

[The four studies above correlate the poems to the writer's life and outlook; they offer usefully different assessments of what his central influences have been.]

MORGAN, E. (1976) *Hugh MacDiarmid*. Harlow, Longman.

[A brief introduction in the British Council *Writers and their Work* series.]

WRIGHT, G. (1977) *MacDiarmid. An Illustrated Biography*, Edinburgh, Gordon Wright Publishing.

[A large format book with many excellent photographs.]

This is not a complete list of periodicals but the following numbers offered special 'MacDiarmid' issues which contain excellent essays on the poet:

AGENDA (Autumn–Winter, 1967–8). W. Cookson (Ed.). 'Double Issue: Hugh MacDiarmid and Scottish Poetry'. London, 5 (4) and 6 (1).

AKROS (April, 1970) D. Glen (Ed.) 'Special Hugh MacDiarmid Issue', Preston, 5 (13–14).

(August, 1977). 'Special Double Hugh MacDiarmid Issue'. Preston, 12 (34–35).

SCOTTISH LITERARY JOURNAL (December, 1978). T. Crawford (Ed.) 'Mac-Diarmid Memorial Number'. Aberdeen, 5 (2).

General Bibliography

GRANT, W. and MURISON, D (Eds) (1929–76) The Scottish National Dictionary, Edinburgh.

ISER, W. (1978) *The Act of Reading*, London, Routledge and Kegan Paul.

KERMODE, F. and HOLLANDER, J. (Eds) (1973) *Modern British Literature: The Oxford Anthology of English Literature*, London, Oxford University Press.

LINKLATER, E. (1982) *Magnus Merriman*, Edinburgh, Macdonald. (First published, 1934.)

MACKINNON, D.M. (1974) *The Problem of Metaphysics*, London, Cambridge University Press.

MUIR, E. (1982) *Scott and Scotland*, Edinburgh, Polygon Books.
[First published in 1936, the opinions in this book led to a decisive break with MacDiarmid.]

SHESTOV, L. (1920) *All Things Are Possible*, S.S. Koteliansky (Trans.), London.

(1932) *In Job's Balances*, C. Coventry and C.A. Macartney (Trans.), London.

SKELTON, R. (Ed.) (1964) *Poetry of the Thirties*, Harmondsworth, Penguin.

SMITH, G.G. (1919) *Scottish Literature: Character and Influence*, London, Macmillan.
[A key influence on MacDiarmid's understanding of the Scottish tradition and character.]

WITTIG, K. (1958) *The Scottish Tradition in Literature*, Edinburgh, Oliver and Boyd.
[Develops Smith's thesis with an excellent case for what is unique and powerful in Scots literature.]

Further Reading in Culture and History

DAICHES, D. (Ed.) (1981) *A Companion to Scottish Culture*, London, Edward Arnold.

HARVIE, C. (1977) *Scotland and Nationalism: 1707–1977*, London, Allen and Unwin.

LENMAN, B. (1977) *An Economic History of Modern Scotland, 1660–1976*, London, Batsford.

MACAULAY, D. (1976) *Modern Scottish Gaelic Poems*, Edinburgh, Southside.
[An anthology of Gaelic poems with the authors' own versions in English as well.]

MURISON, D. (1977) *The Guid Scots Tongue*, Edinburgh, William Blackwood.
[A short, scholarly and most readable introduction to the Scots language, by the editor of the *Scottish National Dictionary*.]
MURRAY, I. and TAIT, B. (1984) *Ten Modern Scottish Novels*, Aberdeen, Aberdeen University Press.
DONNELLY, I; HEARN, S; NORQUAY, G; CALDER, A (1984) *Scottish Literature: A Study Guide*, Edinburgh, the Open University in Scotland.
ROYLE, T. (1983) *The Macmillan Companion to Scottish Literature*, London, Macmillan.
THOMSON, D. (Ed.) (1983) *A Companion to Gaelic Scotland*, Oxford, Blackwell.
(1974) *An Introduction to Gaelic Poetry*, London, Gollancz.
WATSON, R. (1984) *The Literature of Scotland*, London, Macmillan.

Appendix A

A Note on Books, Scots and the Glossary

The page references in this study refer to Michael Grieve and W.R. Aitken (Eds) *Hugh MacDiarmid Complete Poems 1920–1976*, 2 Vols., London, Martin Brian and O'Keeffe, 1978. In 1985, Penguin Books published a second edition in paperback, incorporating a few additional corrections and poems. Page references are the same.

MacDiarmid sprinkles his Scots with apostrophes which, strictly speaking, should not be there. Thus the Scots for *have* is *hae* and it does not have a dropped *v* as the form *ha'e* would suggest. Nevertheless the poet's own usage must stand, and it does have the advantage that it will suggest the more familiar English form of the words to readers who are new to Scots. If you are stuck, try to say the words aloud, as this often helps.

For the quotations used in this study I have given a glossary in parallel with the text itself. This is the least intrusive way to gloss, and a moment's thought will make it clear which word is given for which. A semi-colon separates different words in the order in which they occur in the line. Thus 'I love the rumpus' is given in Scots and glossed as follows:

I lo'e the stishie   love; rumpus

Here are some of the more commonly used Scots words with notes on their pronunciation, though of course this varies in different parts of Scotland.

A'	as in 'far' or 'saw'	all
	found in ANA'	and all
	A'THIN'	everything
	AVA'	at all
CA'	as in 'father' or 'hall'	to call; urge; drive, as in
	found in CA' CANNY	driving sheep or a
	go carefully	grindstone.
EE, pl.EEN	as in 'flee'	eye, eyes
FA'	as in 'father' or 'saw'	fall; befall
	found in FAIR FA' TO YE	bless you; good luck
FOU'	as in 'you'	drunk
FU'	as in 'you'	full

GIN	as in 'begin'	if; whether; by the time
	found in	
	GIN I WERE GOD	if I were God
GANG; GAED;	GAED as in 'aid'	go; went; gone
GANE	GANE as in 'pain'	
GAR; GAR'd	as in 'guard'	to make (as in cause or
	found in	compel);
	GAR'D YE GRUE	made you shudder
LO'E	as in 'grew'	love
MAUN	as in 'lawn'	must
	found in I MAUN GANG	I must go
MUCKLE	as in 'buckle'	large, big, bulky
'NETH	as in 'underneath'	beneath, below
OWRE	as in 'flower'	over; too
	found in OWRE MUCKLE	too big
SIC;SICNA	as in 'sick';–NA as in 'nut'	such, such a
SYNE	as in 'sign'	then, since then; ago
'UD	as in 'depart*ed*'	would
YON	as in 'don' or 'yawn'	that, those

For a collected glossary of Scots words, see the word-leet in Appendix B.

Appendix B

A Glossary of Scots Words

With acknowledgements to the *Scottish National Dictionary*, W. Grant and D. Murison (Eds).

A' all
to ABAW to astonish, to abash
ABUNE above
A'E, ANE one, single
AFORE before
AGLEY awry, off-course
AIBLINS perhaps
AINCE once
A'THING everything
AULD old
AYE always
BAIRN child
BARLEY a truce, a rest from play
BARLEY BREE whisky
to BARM to ferment
BAWAW scornful look
BAWSUNT a white streak as on the face of an animal
BEGOOD begun
BENMAIST uttermost
BLAEBERRIES bilberries
BODY a person
BONNY beautiful, handsome, fine
BOUK body, carcase, bulk
to BOUK to swell up, increase bulk
to BRAIRD to sprout up, germinate
to BREENGE to rush recklessly
BUIRDLY well-built, stalwart
BURN stream

to CA' to call, urge, or to drive as in sheep or a millwheel
CAMSTEERIE perverse, unmanageable
CANNA cannot
CANNY careful, cautious, shrewd
CARLE fellow, bloke
CARLINE old woman, hag
CHITTERIN' shivering
CHUCKIE-STANES small pebbles
CLINTS cliffs
to COUP to overturn
COURAGE BAG scrotum
CRAW crow
CREEL basket
CREESH fat, flesh
to CRINE to shrivel
DAFFIN' frolicking
to DING to dash (p.t.DUNG)
DOITED crazed, idiotic
DOON down
DOUP backside, buttocks
to DROB to prick (as needle)
EE(N) eye(s)
EEMIS ill-poised, wobbling
EIDENT continually busy
ENEUCH enough
ESS ash
FA' fall
FAR'ER further
to FASH to trouble
FEGS faith! (exclamation)

FELL cruel; acute; remarkable
FELL LIKE extremely like
FOU drunk
FU' full
GALLIMAUFRY hotch-potch,
     ragout
GALLUS tough, impudent
to GANG to go
to GAR to make, to oblige to
GEG a token, a toy
to GIE to give
GI'EN given
GIE'D gave
GIN if; whether; by time that
GLISK glimpse
GLIT slime, sperm
GLOWER stare, scowl
GORBLIN unfledged bird
GOUSTROUS blustering, stormy
GOWD gold
to HA'E to have
HALIKET wild, giddy,
     irresponsible
HARNS brains
to HAUD to hold
HERT heart
to HOUK to dig
HOWLET owl
HYNE AWA' far away
I' in
ILKA each, every
ILK'ANE each one
ILL-FAUR'D ill-favoured, ugly
INBY within, inside
INGANGS entrails, guts
INTILL into or inside
KAIM cock's comb; hillcrest
to KECKLE to cackle
to KELTER to tilt or waver
to KEN to know
KENT to know
UNKENT unknown
to KITTLE to tickle; rouse up
LAIGH; LAIGHER low, lower
LANG long
LASS, LASSIE girl
LICHT light
LICHT-LOOKIN' light-looking;
     of no consequence
LIDDENIN' resounding, echoing

LIFT sky
to LIG to lie
LINT-WHITE white as flax
to LO'E to love
LORN longing
to LOUP to jump, leap
LOURD heavy
LOWE flame, blaze, gleam
LOWN hushed, undisturbed
to LOWSE to turn loose
LUG ear
MAIR, MAIST more, most
MAUN must
MIDDEN farmyard dungheap
MUCKLE big, large, bulky
NAE no
'NETH beneath
OCHT anything
OOR our; hour
OOTBY close outside
OWRE over; too
PADDLE-DOO frog
PANASH (hat-plume) brave
     gesture
PEERIE spinning-top
PEERIEWEERIE very small sound
PUDDOCK frog
QUEAN lass, young woman,
     wench
QUHITHER quiver, beam
RAIM-PIG cream jar or jug
to RAX to stretch, reach, strain
REEK smoke
REISTIT dried
REVURE scornful; dark gloomy
     (a word of doubtful
     authenticity)
RIACH dun-coloured
RIBIE tall with little foliage
RICHT right
RIMPIN a lean cow
RINGLE-EE a wall eye
ROON' round
to ROOST to roost
ROOST rust; by extension: rough
     raucous
SAE so
SAVIN' unless, except
SCOUTH scope, liberty
to SCUD to lash past

to SCUNNER to disgust
SCUNNER disgust
SHAIDA shadow
SIC, SICNA such, such a
SICCAR sure, certain
to MAK' SICCAR to make sure
SILLER silver
SKATE skate (fish)
to SKINKLE to shine, glitter
SLIDDERY slithery
SMA'-BOUKIT shrunk;
    small-bodied
SOON' sound, smooth
to S. A PEERIE to spin a top
to SPALE to melt, run down
SPALIN' guttering
SPAULD shoulder
to SPEIR to ask about
to SPLAIRGE to splatter, splash
    out
SPREIT spirit
STANG paroxysm
to STAP to stuff
STERT start
STISHIE stir, commotion
STOUR dust; water driven by
    wind
STRAUCHT straight
SUNE soon
SUNER sooner
SYNE since; then
SIN'SYNE since then
TAE to; too (also toe)
TAED toad
THUNNER thunder

UNCO anything unusual or
    prodigous; very
'UD would
WAE woe
WAESOME woeful
WANRESTFU' restless
WANCHANCY unlucky, ill-fated
WARL' world
WATERGAW indistinct or broken
    rainbow
WAUGH bad, disgusting to smell
    or taste; morally worthless
WECHT weight
WEEL well (as in well done)
WHA who
WHATNA what (kind of)
WHAUR where
WHIGMALEERIES whims,
    fancies, fantastic
    ornamentations
WHILES at times
to WHUDDER to make a
    whizzing rushing noise (hence
    WHUDS)
WHUMMLIN' tumbling
WILL AND WILYART wrong
    and wilful
WORD-LEET word-list, glossary
WROCHT wrought
YON that, those
'YONT beyond
YOUKY itchy
YOWDENDRIFT snow blown up
    from ground.

Index